SENTENCE STRUCTURE

IN THE SAME SERIES

Editor: Richard Hudson

SENTENCE STRUCTURE

Nigel Fabb

London and New York

First published 1994
by Routledge
11 New Fetter Lane, London EC4P 4EE

Simultaneously published in the USA and Canada
by Routledge
29 West 35th Street, New York, NY 10001

© 1994 Nigel Fabb

Typeset in Times Ten by Florencetype Limited
Kewstoke, Avon

Printed and bound in Great Britain by
T.J. Press (Padstow) Ltd, Padstow, Cornwall

Printed on acid-free paper

British Library Cataloguing in Publication Data
A catalogue record for this book is available from the British Library

Library of Congress Cataloging in Publication Data
A catalogue record for this book is available from the Library of Congress

ISBN 0-415-08569-1

CONTENTS

USING THIS BOOK

This book can be used for a course in English grammar or an introductory course in linguistics (specifically, an introduction to syntax). It focuses on the foundational issues of identification and solution of problems in sentence structure. It is not centrally concerned with teaching traditional grammatical terminology (you can see exactly what it does teach by looking at the index), and it avoids reference to the details of linguistic theory (except in unit 12).

The book can be used for independent study, though you will find it helpful to discuss your answers to exercises with someone else.

It is important to do the exercises. Some of them introduce material which is not otherwise found in the text, and later exercises may build on the results of earlier ones. This is particularly true of the exercises on English, all of which you should complete. The exercises on other languages (many using the final corpora) are less central to the argument of the book, but provide a breadth and richness to your understanding of sentence structure which will be essential if you plan to do any further work in linguistics.

The exercises range from quite easy to quite difficult; some help you to consolidate and test your understanding of the unit you have read, while others ask you to explore problems which have been a source of difficulty and controversy even for fully developed linguistic theories.

Write down the answers and draw the tree structures (rather than just imagining what the answer might be); solving problems in sentence structure is often a matter of putting something down on a page, and then examining it.

You should not need to do any supplementary or background reading while you are reading and working through this book. At the end, we provide a list of more advanced or more detailed books which you might turn to once you have finished this one.

ACKNOWLEDGEMENTS

Thanks to Woohak Lee, Toh Guat Choon, Kon Yoon How, Mairi John Blackings, Wan Faiezah bt. Megat Noordin, Yasmin bt. Osman, Rajathilagam a/l Krishnan, Deborah Cameron, Helen Reid-Thomas, Janet Fabb and the Strathclyde University students on whom this book was tested. Earlier versions of this book were read with great care by, among others, Andrew Ing, Edward Waldron, Nurul Basher, Jillbob Newton, and the series editor, Dick Hudson. Their comments and criticisms were invaluable; any mistakes which remain are mine. Finally I should acknowledge the many unnamed linguists whose ideas and discoveries are the basis for this book.

ABBREVIATIONS

A	adjective
Adv	adverb
AdvP	adverb phrase
AP	adjective phrase
art	article
c.c.	coordinating conjunction
cl.	classifier
deg	degree modifier
dem	demonstrative
inf	infinitive marker
N	noun/pronoun
neg	negation
NP	noun phrase
num	numeral
P	preposition/postposition
PP	preposition phrase/postposition phrase
Q	quantifier
S	sentence
s.c.	subordinating conjunction
V	verb
V_{aux}	auxiliary verb
V_{mod}	modal verb
VP	verb phrase

PHRASES

1

> A single written sentence may stand for two different sentence structures, each having a different meaning. The structures differ because the words are grouped into different phrases. Phrases can be discovered by replacement and movement of sequences of words.

In this book we look at how sentences are put together. We try to answer these questions: what evidence is there for sentence structure? What is sentence structure for? And what kinds of sentence structure exist? Here are some of the reasons for thinking that it is worth trying to answer these questions:

- Language is central to our lives, one of the things which makes us human. Understanding any aspect of language helps us understand more about ourselves.
- All humans have language, but we are divided from each other by the differences between our languages. By understanding more about each language, we can better handle the similarities and differences between our languages – for example, understanding more about language may help you learn a language.
- Language is used for many purposes: to communicate, to write literature or perform songs, to persuade. Understanding an application of language becomes easier once we understand how language is put together.
- You and I both know English: but what exactly does 'knowing English' mean? – It must, in part, mean 'knowing the sentence structures of English'. So investigating sentence structure means investigating a kind of knowledge which we cannot uncover simply by looking inside ourselves.

We return to some of these issues – particularly the last one – in the final unit. But for the most part this book will be devoted to laying the foundations.

We have looked at some reasons for being interested in sentence structure. But what *is* sentence structure? There are three essential aspects: the constituency of a sentence (the units into which it can be divided, such as words and phrases), the labelling of those units (with labels like 'noun' or 'adjective phrase'), and the ordering of those units relative to one another (for example, what comes before the verb, and what comes after: a crucial question in determining a sentence's meaning). We begin here with constituency. The constituents of something are the units out of which it is made. A word is an obvious example of a constituent of a sentence. A less obvious type of constituent is a PHRASE, which is a sequence of words which form a coherent group. This unit looks at some reasons for saying that words are grouped into phrases.

Phrase

Meaning and phrase structure

Ambiguous

We begin by looking at the meaning of a sentence, and by focusing on a sentence (1) which is AMBIGUOUS – that is, it has more than one possible meaning.

> (1) I was reading the letter to John.

Before you go on, decide what the two possible meanings of this sentence are.

This sentence might mean:

> (a) that there was a letter addressed to John which I was reading (perhaps to myself).

Or it might mean:

> (b) that there was a letter (to me, perhaps) which I was reading aloud to John.

We might say that there are two different sentences which look exactly the same (they both look like (1)), though they mean different things.

We work out the structure of a sentence in order to understand it. In this case, the most obvious structural aspects fail to distinguish the two different sentences: they both have the same words in the same order. So we need to look for a structural difference between them which is not so immediately obvious. This difference is to be found in the different ways in which the words are grouped into phrases.

> (2) I was reading (the letter to John.)

> (3) I was reading (the letter) (to John.)

In (2) the sequence *the letter to John* forms a single phrase, while in (3) *the letter* forms one phrase and *to John* forms a separate one. We can say that there are two sentence structures ((2) and (3)) which correspond to a single written sentence (1).

What evidence can we give that there are two different ways of structuring (1) into phrases? We will now see that there are two basic tests which are based on the fact that if a phrase exists it can be replaced or moved.

We'll start with replacement. The word *it* can replace one of two sequences of words in (1), either *the letter to John*, giving (4), or *the letter*, giving (5).

Replacement and phrase structure

>   (4) I was reading it.

>   (5) I was reading it to John.

We have taken an ambiguous sentence, (1), and turned it into two alternative non-ambiguous sentences. In terms of the two meanings we distinguished, (4) now has just meaning (a), which corresponds to the structure in (2): *it* has replaced a single phrase. And (5) has just meaning (b), and corresponds to the structure in (3): again, *it* has replaced a single phrase. The use of *it* to decide what sequence of words constitutes a whole phrase relies on a particular test for phrase structure:

> THE REPLACEMENT TEST FOR PHRASE STRUCTURE
> If a sequence of words can be replaced by a single word, they may form a phrase.

The replacement test for phrase structure

In the example we chose, we used a word called a 'pronoun' to replace the phrase. Other pronouns are *she, he, they, her, our*, and so on. We discuss them again on p. 46. Not every kind of phrase can be replaced by a pronoun. The replacement test can also use a word chosen from the phrase which it is replacing, as in the following example, where *some women wearing hard hats* is replaced by *women*, not a pronoun but a word chosen from the phrase:

>   (6) I saw some women wearing hard hats.

>   (7) I saw women.

Note that replacement works as a test only if the meaning stays roughly the same.

Movement and phrase structure

Movement gives the same results as replacement, for sentence (1). If we move *the letter to John* as a group, we end up with a sentence which has meaning (a):

>   (8) The letter to John was being read by me.

If on the other hand we move the pair of words *the letter* on their own, we get meaning (b). This corresponds to the structure in (3), since it involves the idea that *the letter* is a phrase on its own:

>   (9) The letter was being read by me to John.

Notice that we get the same result if we move *to John* on its own; only meaning (b) remains (as we would expect, given that again we are manipulating specifically the structure in (3)).

(10) To John I was reading the letter.

These activities depend on the second basic test for phrase structure:

The movement test for phrase structure

THE MOVEMENT TEST FOR PHRASE STRUCTURE
If a sequence of words can be moved as a group, they may form a phrase.

There are sometimes a number of different options for where and how a phrase can be moved.

(11) Five old fish saw three young crabs.

This can be changed into:

(12) Three young crabs were seen by five old fish.

(13) It was three young crabs that the five old fish saw.

(14) It was five old fish that saw the three young crabs.

Notice that in (12) both phrases have been moved, swapping positions:

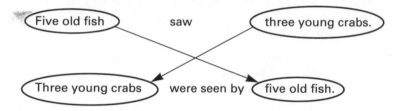

Applying the tests

We have seen two tests for the phrase structure of a sentence. Using these tests, we can now look at some more sentences, and look for phrases in them.

For sentence (15) we can show that *very happy with his new bathroom* is a phrase.

(15) John seems very happy with his new bathroom.

First we apply the replacement test, substituting just the word *happy* for the sequence of words:

(16) John seems happy.

Notice that *happy* is not a pronoun; in this case, what we have done is to pick a word from the phrase which somehow sums up the phrase, and replace the phrase by the word. Next, we try the movement test:

(17) Very happy with his new bathroom is how John seems.

This gives the same results.

Now we'll do the same with (18), testing whether *in five or ten minutes* groups together as a phrase.

(18) He will be arriving in five or ten minutes.

We apply the replacement test, substituting *soon* for *in five or ten minutes*:

(19) He will be arriving soon.

And we apply the movement test, putting *in five or ten minutes* at the beginning of the sentence:

(20) In five or ten minutes he will be arriving.

Now consider sentence (15) again.

(15) John seems very happy with his new bathroom.

We can show that *very happy with his new bathroom* is a phrase. But we can also show that *with his new bathroom* is a phrase inside the larger phrase. The movement test shows this – we can put *with his new bathroom* at the beginning of the sentence:

(21) With his new bathroom John seems very happy.

Furthermore, we can show that *his new bathroom* is a phrase inside *that* phrase – it can for example be replaced by *it*:

(22) John seems very happy with it.

So we can see that the constituency or 'phrase structure' of (15) is quite complicated, with phrases inside phrases:

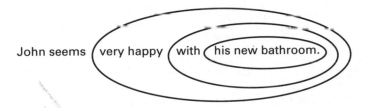

John seems (very happy (with (his new bathroom.)))

Working out the phrase structure of a sentence consists largely of working out how words group into phrases, and working out how phrases fit into other phrases, as in the example above.

Let's briefly review what we have done. We have seen that sequences of words can be manipulated by replacing them or moving them; we call these sequences 'phrases'. The replacement and movement tests discover the phrase structure of a sentence, otherwise hidden from immediate view. We have seen that different ways of grouping words into phrases correspond to sentences with different meanings. So this suggests that one of the characteristics of a sentence which makes it have a particular meaning is the way in which its words are grouped into phrases: that is, the phrase structure contributes to the meaning of the sentence. So we can see why phrases are an essential component of a sentence: they have a role in enabling a sentence to have a particular meaning.

WHY PHRASES?

Acceptability judgements

Sometimes we apply a test and find that the sentence we end up with is unacceptable. For example, we might want to find out if *very happy with* is a phrase in (15), repeated here:

(15) John seems very happy with his new bathroom.

If we apply the movement test, we get:

(23) *Very happy with John seems his new bathroom.

A test is just as useful whether it ends up with an acceptable sentence or an unacceptable sentence. The unacceptable sentence in this case suggests that *very happy with* is *not* a phrase: so it tells us something. So we have to be interested in unacceptable sentences.

Without the distinction between acceptable and unacceptable sentences, it is difficult to analyse sentence structure. There is, however, a problem about the notion of acceptability, which we should mention. Making these decisions about acceptability is sometimes straightforward, in the sense that all speakers of a language would agree. But there are complications. In poetry, for example, there is a wider tolerance for odd sentences – that is, a sentence which might normally seem unacceptable might nevertheless be acceptable in a poem. Then again, someone might use English in a way which someone else considers to be 'bad English' or perhaps 'slang'; people will not always agree on acceptability (we will not take any sides on issues in these debates which are more about social power than about sentence structure as such). All of this means that the notion of 'acceptability' is a complicated one, which needs to be handled with care. The way we will use the notion of acceptability in this book is to say that a sentence of English is acceptable if we could find a native speaker of English who might accept it. We will call such a sentence a GRAMMATICAL SENTENCE. A sentence which no one would accept is called an UNGRAMMATICAL SENTENCE and we write an asterisk at the front of it, as in (23). We return to these topics in unit 12.

Grammatical sentence
Ungrammatical sentence

EXERCISES

1.   The woman from London bought the bookcase for her friends from the antique seller on Friday morning.

(a) Write three different sentences which could mean the same as this, but where you have replaced a phrase with a word (or several phrases with several words).

(b) Write three different sentences which could mean the same as this, but where you have moved a phrase (or several phrases).

(c) On the basis of your answers to (a) and (b) suggest how the sentence is broken up into phrases (remember that a phrase may be found inside another phrase).

2. The following sentences are ambiguous: each sentence has two possible meanings. The ambiguity comes from the possibility of grouping the words in two different ways.

(1) I wrapped the present for John.

(2) He felt the pain in his shoulder.

(3) I looked up the passage.

(4) I once wrote an article on this table.

(5) The nurse fed the cat in the kitchen.

(a) Putting circles around the groups, show what the two different groupings are for each sentence. `

(b) Show how the tests of replacement and movement prove that your groupings are correct for each meaning of each sentence.

---

3. The Korean sentences ((1)–(5)) below all mean roughly the same (and are all acceptable). They all mean 'Yesterday the old man gave Peter's green ball to the children'. The words have been put into different orders, but despite the reordering some groups of words remain stuck together in phrases.

Circle what you think the phrases are in the first of these sentences (1), on the basis of the evidence provided by the (reordered) other sentences.

(1) eaje ke noin-i chorok saek kong-el peter-ei aidel-ege ju-eatsepnida

(2) ke noin-i eaje chorok saek kong-el peter-ei aidel-ege ju-eatsepnida

(3) eaje ke noin-i peter-ei aidel-ege chorok saek kong-el ju-eatsepnida

(4) chorok saek kong-el ke noin-i peter-ei aidel-ege eaje ju-eatsepnida

(5) peter-ei aidel-ege ke noin-i eaje chorok saek kong-el ju-eatsepnida

(This activity demonstrates that it is possible to find the phrase structure of a sentence without knowing much about the meaning of the individual phrases. Korean is a language which allows fairly free word order, but you will have noticed that one part is always final – this is the verb: here, *ju-eatsepnida*, meaning 'gave'.)

4.

house   white

it   Peter's   I

be   easy

thought

would   to   recognize

Make an acceptable English sentence from this jumble of words. As you do so, write down a description of:

    (a) how you know how to group the words together into phrases; try to do this without mentioning word classes ('verb' etc.), even if you know them;

    (b) how you decide how the phrases are ordered to make a sentence; try to do this without mentioning phrase classes (such as 'noun phrase'), even if you know them.

---

5. Sometimes every speaker of English will agree that a particular sentence is unacceptable (these are the ones which we mark in this book with an asterisk). But many sentences are liable to provoke disagreement, sometimes quite angry disagreement. Each sentence listed below (1)–(12) would be considered unacceptable as a sentence of written English by someone (perhaps everyone). Because the notion of acceptability is important in this book, this exercise gives you an opportunity to explore some of the questions relating to it.

    (a) Look at the following sentences, and list any which you think *no* user of English would accept.

    (b) For each of the other sentences, explain why people might disagree as to whether it is acceptable. You might need to consider issues of social class, regional and national difference, formality, politics, belief, etc.

The first one has been done for you, to indicate the kind of answer you should give (it is discussed under (b) since some users would accept it):

    (1) He said to leave. And I did as he said.

Sample answer: Some people take the view (supported by influential writers of style manuals) that a sentence should not begin with the word *and*. Many writers, however, use *and* at the beginning of a sentence (sometimes specifically to get an effect of informality or spokenness).

(2) Man is different from the other animals because of his rich culture.

(3) The sun goes round the earth.

(4) I didnae see it.

(5) Whom did they give it to?

(6) I and he want particularly to see the ballgame.

(7) He has might gone.

(8) I am knowing the answer.

(9) Dog shit is a serious nuisance to pedestrians.

(10) Dear is the memory of our wedded lives.

(11) The Decadent artists had Oscar Wilde on their head.

(12) This plant can not be put next to that table.

---

6. The following longer exercise requires you to work with the four corpora ('corpuses') at the end of the book. As you work, you will find it useful to put word-for-word translations under the sentences (this slows you down, but it will be increasingly useful as you go through the book). You may find that you can't translate all the words to start with (for example the Malay word *telah* may prove difficult); leave these problems – you will get a chance to focus on them in later chapters. Read 'How to use the four corpora which follow' (pp. 125–6) before doing this exercise.

The purpose of this exercise is to give you further practice at using the tests for phrases, and to demonstrate some of the differences in phrase structure between different languages. By comparing sentences in a language which mean similar things it is possible to detect the presence of phrases, because phrases can be moved or replaced. The following sets of sentences demonstrate the presence of phrases. For each language's set, say what evidence there is for the presence of phrases in the sentence. We have given a sample answer to (a):

(a) Chinese: compare B1, 2, 3

Sample answer: *sai louchai* can be replaced by *pinko*, suggesting that it is a phrase. *kó teeu tai yu* can be replaced by *matye*, suggesting that it is a phrase.

(b) Chinese: compare C1, C2
(c) Madi: compare B1, B2, B4–6
(d) Madi: compare C3 with C4 and C1 with C2 (make sure you read the notes at the beginning of the Madi section)
(e) Madi: compare A2, L1 and L2; compare A3, L3 and L4
(f) Malay: compare C1, C2

(g) Malay: compare B1–5
(h) Malay: compare A1–3 with L1–3
(i)   Tamil: compare A1, A2
(j)   Tamil: compare B1, B3 (replacement)
(k) Tamil: compare B1–10 (movement)

WORD CLASS

2

> The position of a word depends on its word class. There are different classes of phrase, which contain different word classes.

WORD ORDER INSIDE THE PHRASE: THE NEED TO CLASSIFY WORDS

Now that we know how to decide for a particular sentence how its words are grouped into phrases, we will look inside the phrases. We begin by focusing on word order inside the phrase.

Despite their having the same phrase structure (indicated in part by circling), sentence (1) is grammatical but (2) is not.

(1) I saw (the white house.)

(2) *I saw (the house white.)

The ungrammaticality of (2) apparently comes from the order of the words inside the phrase. This isn't a problem that just applies to the words *house* and *white*, as we can see by substituting any of thousands of other words:

(3) I saw the big elephant.

(4) *I saw the elephant big.

We can only begin to explain what is wrong with (2) if we talk in terms of word class. A WORD CLASS is a collection of words which have characteristics in common and which are given a collective name; some examples are 'noun', 'verb', 'adjective', 'article'.

Word class

In this case, the characteristics in common relate to the order of words, and this is one of the basic reasons for identifying words as belonging to different classes. So let's assume two classes, ADJECTIVE and NOUN, with the following members (among others: these are very large classes):

Adjective
Noun

11

Some English adjectives	white, big, new, small, broken, happy, renewed, astonishing, beautiful
Some English nouns	house, elephant, wall, bucket, book, window, child, hope, news, mountain

(You may notice that we have not *defined* either adjective or noun. There is a reason for this, which we'll return to on p. 38.)

Armed with this classification we can now make a generalization about English phrases, which is this:

> English generalization 1
> Inside a phrase an adjective precedes a noun.

Generalization

A GENERALIZATION is a statement which is supposed to be generally true; for example, this statement should be true for any sequence of adjective and noun in English – the adjective should always come before the noun. Example (4) is ungrammatical because it breaks or violates the generalization.

We can also classify the word *the*, which comes at the beginning (rather than, for example, at the end) of the phrase. *The* belongs to a very small word class of ARTICLES; the only other member is *a* (or *an*, an alternative form of *a*). Here's a generalization to get started with:

Article

> English generalization 2
> An article comes at the beginning of a phrase.

The purpose of our generalizations, remember, is to begin to work out how word class relates to word order.

Here are some examples of phrases with adjective, noun and article indicated (when present). Notice that in each case, the adjective comes before the noun, and the article comes at the beginning, just as generalizations 1 and 2 claim:

article	adjective	noun
the	broken	window
a		child
	renewed	hope
an	astonishing	report
the	beautiful	mountain

A difference between languages

One of the useful things about our generalizations is that they allow us to make a very specific comparison between English and another language. For example, while in English the adjective comes before the noun, this is not true in Welsh, as the following examples show:

(5) llyfr   newydd   Mary
    book   new   Mary
    'Mary's new book'

(6) y   tŷ   gwyn
    the   house   white
    'the white house'

So in comparison with English generalization 1 we could have:

Welsh generalization 1
In a phrase an adjective follows a noun.

Word order inside a phrase is one of the major structural ways in which languages can differ from each other. Notice that the article comes at the beginning of the phrase, just like in English. But there are languages in which the article comes at the end of the phrase, as is shown by the following example from the African language Fon:

(7) vi   o
    child the
    'the child'

This, too, can be the basis of a generalization, which we can compare with English generalization 2:

Fon generalization
An article comes at the end of a phrase.

The generalization that we invented for English word order applies to words *inside* the same phrase. It doesn't work if we try to apply it *across* phrases, as the following exercise shows.

**The general-
izations about
word order do
not apply *across*
phrases**

✐ **EXERCISE**

Circle the phrases in the following sentences. Use the tests of substitution (e.g. try substituting with *it* or *its*) to prove that your circling of phrases is correct:

(8) I saw the white house.

(9) I saw the house's white walls.

(10) I painted the house white.

Do this exercise before going any further.

The crucial differences between the phrases are shown below:

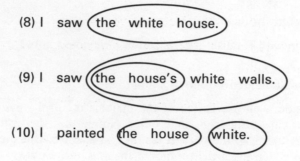

(8) I saw the white house.

(9) I saw the house's white walls.

(10) I painted the house white.

The replacement test can be used to distinguish the different structures of the three sentences; in each case, we use *it* to replace the phase containing *house*:

(11) I saw it.   (*compare with 8*)

(12) I saw its white walls.   (*compare with 9*)

(13) I painted it white.   (*compare with 10*)

The point of these examples is that in (9) and in (10) the noun (*house*) comes *before* (not after) the adjective (*white*). But they are in different phrases; in both cases, the noun *house* is in a separate phrase from the adjective *white*. So we can make statements about word order like 'In English the adjective comes before the noun' only if we specify that those statements are true inside phrases, but not between phrases.

The degree modifier

We now look at another class of word, exemplified by *very*. We'll call it a DEGREE MODIFIER.

Some English degree modifiers very, rather, quite, somewhat, too, pretty

These words are called degree modifiers because they indicate the degree of something; compare the difference in meaning which you get by choosing different degree modifiers in *very hot*, *quite hot*, and *too hot*.

Let's look at where a degree modifier goes.

(14) I bought the very small bucket.

We know that *the very small bucket* is a phrase (it can be substituted by *it* for example, as in *I bought it*). And we can see that *inside* this phrase, *very small* is a phrase of its own:

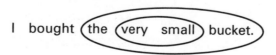

I bought the very small bucket.

We can show this by reordering the sentence to show that *very small* sticks together as a unit:

> (15) I bought the bucket which was very small.

So we can see that *very* goes at the beginning of a phrase. Here's the generalization:

> English generalization 3
> A degree modifier comes at the beginning of a phrase.

So a degree modifier like *very* goes at the beginning of a phrase, and an article like *the* also goes at the beginning of a phrase (English generalization 2, p. 12). But they are not interchangeable, which means that they do not actually go in the same place, as the generalizations incorrectly imply:

There are different sorts of phrase

> (16) *I bought (very (the small) bucket.

What this illustrates is that there are two sorts of phrase here: two different PHRASE CLASSES. We can put phrases into classes just as we can put words into classes.

Phrase class

Very small is a class of phrase called an 'adjective phrase', while *the very small bucket* is a class of phrase called a 'noun phrase':

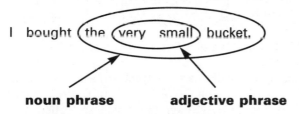

noun phrase   adjective phrase

Thus we can make our generalizations more specific:

> English generalization 2 (revised)
> An article comes at the beginning of a noun phrase.
> English generalization 3 (revised)
> A degree modifier comes at the beginning of an adjective phrase.

Notice that there is another change which we must make. This one is more subtle, but is necessary. Earlier we said that an adjective precedes a noun (in English). Now we see that in fact it is the adjective *phrase* which precedes the noun; the adjective phrase contains an adjective (and so by derivation, the adjective precedes the noun). So we need to change generalization 1 as well:

> English generalization 1 (revised)
> Inside a phrase an adjective phrase precedes a noun.

For each of our generalizations, we have had to revise our first versions. This is typical of the kind of work involved in investigating sentence structure: by trial and error we build an increasingly accurate picture.

Phrase classes are named after word classes. In this book we will use four different phrase classes: noun phrase, adjective phrase, preposition phrase (named after the word class preposition) and adverb phrase (named after the word class adverb). In unit 11 we investigate whether there is in addition a verb phrase. In unit 3 we investigate the relation between a phrase class and a word class.

TREE STRUCTURE DIAGRAMS

We can show more clearly the various claims we are making about words and phrases by drawing a TREE STRUCTURE diagram, like the following:

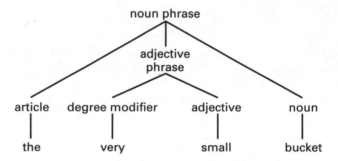

This kind of diagram is called a tree structure because it looks a bit like an upside-down tree (with the root at the top). You might notice that it resembles 'family tree' diagrams, which are called 'trees' for the same reason.

We will be using this kind of diagram from now onwards. In order to simplify the writing of the diagrams, we use abbreviated ways of referring to the different word classes and phrase classes. So we would normally write the diagram like this:

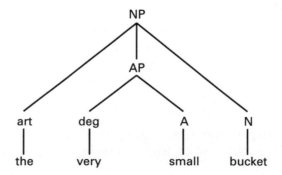

(A list showing the different abbreviations for word classes is given on p. *x*; adding 'P' indicates a phrase – NP = noun phrase for example.)

✐ **EXERCISES**

1. Here are six noun phrases ((1)–(6)) some of which contain adjective phrases. The word classes have been written below each word.

Draw tree structures for these phrases.

(1) a   rather   ugly   hat
    article   *degree modifier*   *adjective*   *noun*

(2) an   elephant
    article   *noun*

(3) a   recent   proposal
    article   *adjective*   *noun*

(4) a   pretty   risky   decision
    article   *degree modifier*   *adjective*   *noun*

(5) the   airport
    article   *noun*

(6) a   successful   bid
    article   *adjective*   *noun*

2. The following noun phrase is slightly different from the ones we have seen before.

the long hot summer

(a) Explain what is different about this noun phrase.
(b) Draw a tree structure for it and justify the phrase structure which you give.
(c) Do any of the generalizations in this unit have to be changed in order to account for this noun phrase? If not, explain why. If so, suggest a new generalization, or change one of the existing ones.

3. This and the next exercise will take somewhat longer to do. They will take you further in an understanding of the different structures of the different languages in the corpus, and are useful preparation for later work. As you do the exercises, keep adding word-for-word translations under the sentences.

For each language in the corpus:

(a) Identify some noun phrases.
(b) Work out which parts in the phrase correspond to: noun, adjective phrase and article. (Note: you may find that there

is no article in a particular language. The adjective phrase
may consist just of the adjective.)

(c) State a generalization about the order of article, adjective
phrase and noun in the noun phrase.

Look particularly at the following examples:

Chinese: A1, A3, D1
Madi: A5 (compare with A1, for example, to begin to work out
the meaning of individual words)
Malay: D3, D4
Tamil: C2, C3, D1, D4, D5

---

4. For Chinese, Madi and Tamil:

(a) Identify some adjective phrases.
(b) Work out which parts in the phrase correspond to adjective
and degree modifier.
(c) What is the order of these parts in the phrase?

Look particularly at the following examples:

Chinese: D8, D9, J1, J2
Madi: D2 (compare with A5)
Tamil: D4, D8–10

PHRASE CLASS AND WORD CLASS

3

The class of a phrase is linked to the classes of the words it contains, particularly its head. This is the basis for various tests for phrase class (which can be turned also into tests for word class).

As we saw in unit 2, the class of a word is closely linked to the class of the phrase which contains it. A degree modifier and an adjective are found in an adjective phrase, while an article and a noun are found in a noun phrase. In this unit we explore further the link between phrase class and word class, and develop some tests which will enable us to work out the class of any word or phrase we are unsure about in any particular sentence.

It's worth exploring for a moment the two difficulties which confront us in working out the class of a word. First, there is a problem which comes from the widespread ambiguity of written English (the same applies to many languages). Consider for example this word:

Why is it sometimes difficult to determine the class of a word?

fish *verb or noun?*

What is its word class?

Try to answer this question before reading any further.

Of course, it was a trick question. You can't always tell the class of the word by looking at it in isolation, and this word in isolation is ambiguous. There are (at least) two different meanings, which correspond to two different word classes. Putting it in a sentence can often clear up the ambiguity. In (1) it is a noun; in (2) it is a verb.

(1) I liked the fish.

(2) I liked to fish.

So this is the first problem about working out the class of the word. A word class can often only be decided by analysing the structure of a sentence.

The second problem is that people do not always agree on what word classes are found in a language. For example, many grammarians think that 'particle' is a type of word class (in this book, we don't claim this – but you have an opportunity to begin to decide for yourself, in exercise 4). Decisions about the structure of a particular sentence are always related to much broader views (which can be argued for or against) about what sentence structure looks like in general. The same basic difficulties apply to all aspects of sentence structure, not just word class: is the general approach right, and is this analysis of this specific sentence right? We will confront this problem again, specifically with regard to whether there is a verb phrase in any English sentence. Many linguists think there is; others think there is not. This is not a matter of personal belief; instead it is a matter of argument. While we do not use a 'verb phrase' for the analyses in this book, we devote unit 11 to some of the arguments which might be made for or against it.

ask a silly question, you get a silly answer *

The internal structure of a phrase

The close relation between word class and phrase class can be used as a way of identifying the class of any particular phrase. Consider, for example, the fact that an article (*the* or *a\an*) appears only in a noun phrase, and appears at the beginning of such a phrase. This means that if we have a phrase which begins with *the*, it must be a noun phrase. We can state the basic idea in the form of a test for phrase class:

The internal structure test for phrase class

THE INTERNAL STRUCTURE TEST FOR PHRASE CLASS
The class of a component of a phrase (or some other aspect of its structure) can indicate the class of the phrase.

There are a number of other word classes which are like articles in that they appear only at the beginning of a noun phrase. These are the demonstratives, numerals and quantifiers. They are discussed in more detail in unit 9, where we look at noun phrases in more detail. Here are some examples from each class:

* There is no objective reality that decides whether there is or is not. It is all just playing with words.

Some English DEMONSTRATIVES	this, that, these, those	**Demonstratives**
Some English NUMERALS	one, thirty, ninety-nine, two hundred and fifty-seven	**Numerals**
Some English QUANTIFIERS	every, some, all, few, most, much, no, many	**Quantifiers**

All these word classes indicate the presence of a noun phrase, because they are always found inside a noun phrase.

There is another sense in which the components of a phrase indicate the class of the phrase. This involves the notion of HEAD of a phrase. Each of the four kinds of phrase are headed by words of the same basic kind. We can state this as a rule:

Head

> THE HEAD RULE
> A phrase of class 'X phrase' contains a word of class 'X' (where X stands for noun, adjective, preposition or adverb).

The head rule

As we'll see, this is a rule that can be broken – it is possible to have headless phrases. But most of the time phrases do have a head; if there is just one word in a phrase it will usually be its head. This match between word and phrase class means that:

(a) if we know the class of a phrase, we know the class of one of the words in it; and conversely,

(b) if we know the class of a word, we know the class of the phrase that contains it.

We will put this to practical use when we draw up some guidelines for working out the tree structures of sentences on pp. 61–2.

The more we know about the possible internal structures of the different classes of phrase, the better equipped we are to identify the class of any particular phrase. For example, we already know something about some typical noun phrase and adjective phrase structures:

(3)
```
    NP
    |
    N
    |
 bananas
```

(4)
```
      NP
     /  \
   art    N
    |     |
   the  bananas
```

(5)
```
       NP
      /  \
     /   AP
    /    |
  art    A    N
   |     |    |
  the   big bananas
```

Some typical noun phrase structures

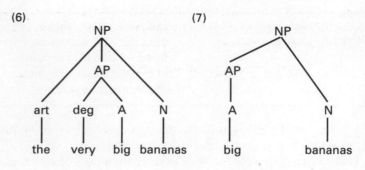

Some typical adjective phrase structures

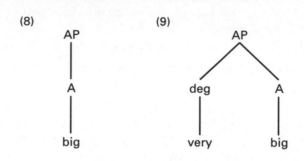

REPLACING A PHRASE

We will see in unit 5 that, to some extent, different phrase classes appear in different places. This will give us another test for phrase class.

The position test for phrase class

THE POSITION TEST FOR PHRASE CLASS
Each class of phrase appears in certain positions, and not in others.

One of the consequences of this is that if a phrase can be replaced by another phrase, particularly if the meaning remains more or less the same, then it is possible that the two phrases are of the same class:

The replacement test for phrase class

THE REPLACEMENT TEST FOR PHRASE CLASS
A phrase can be replaced by another phrase of the same class.

We have already seen an example of this. In unit 1 we saw that a pronoun can replace a phrase; specifically, a pronoun typically replaces a noun phrase. The reason for this is that a pronoun is a type of noun, and is contained in a noun phrase. So when a pronoun replaces a noun phrase what is actually happening is that one noun phrase replaces another. (We will justify the claim that a pronoun is a noun on pp. 46–7.)

This gives a fairly reliable test for whether something is a noun phrase; if a phrase can be replaced by *it*, *he*, *she*, *they*, etc., then it is likely to be a noun phrase. It is not a completely reliable test, though – the noun *there* can replace a preposition phrase, and the noun *it* can replace a sentence; what this means is that if you are in doubt, replacement might be just *one of several* tests you need to try.

Having reviewed various tests which relate phrase class and word class, we will now introduce a new word and phrase class. In sentence (10), *very slowly* is a phrase.

Adverbs and adverb phrases

> (10) I walked to the machine very slowly.

Show by reordering the sentence that *very slowly* is a phrase.

Do this before going on.

We can show that *very* and *slowly* stick together as a phrase because they can be moved around together inside the sentence:

> (11) *Very slowly* I walked to the machine.

> (12) I *very slowly* walked to the machine.

> (13) I walked *very slowly* to the machine.

> (14) I walked to the machine *very slowly*.

So we know that *very slowly* is a phrase, but what kind of phrase is it? It looks a bit like an adjective phrase – for example, it begins with the degree modifier *very*, just like an adjective phrase. But the position test tells us that it is not an adjective phrase. An adjective phrase can appear between an article and a noun (i.e. inside a noun phrase); but *very slowly* cannot:

> (15) *I walked to the *very slowly* machine.

Furthermore, an adjective phrase cannot appear in as many places in the sentence as *very slowly* can. So this is a new type of phrase, with its own distinctive positions. It is called an ADVERB PHRASE, and the head is the ADVERB – here *slowly*. Here are some more adverbs:

**Adverb phrase
Adverb**

Some English adverbs	slowly, quietly, probably, better, fortunately, sadly, fast

Notice that *fast* is one of those many English words which is ambiguous between word class. There are two words with the same form of *fast*: an adjective, as in *a fast car*, and an adverb, as in *he ran fast*.

The internal structure of *very slowly* is like this:

(16)

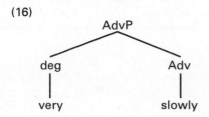

Here are some sentences with adverb phrases in them (italicized):

(17) We walked *quickly* round the block.

(18) *Rather unfortunately,* the fish have all sold out.

(19) *Probably* they went there *very speedily*.

The most striking structural characteristic of adverb phrases is that they can be scattered throughout the sentence.

English adverbs have another striking and obvious characteristic, which is that they have a typical shape: most adverbs end in *-ly*. We will come back to 'word shape' tests on p. 31, where we see that word classes can sometimes be identified by the shape of the words. However, like other tests, this test is not entirely reliable on its own: some adverbs do not end in *-ly* (*fast*, *best*, etc., are examples), and some words end in *-ly* which are *not* adverbs. For example, the word *lovely* is an adjective.

Prepositions and preposition phrases

In the following sentence we have circled all the noun phrases.

(20)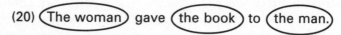

But there is one more phrase which we could also circle.

Show, by reordering the sentence, that there is one more (so far uncircled) phrase (containing several words) in the sentence.

Do this before reading any further.

It is possible to rewrite the sentence in a different order as (21) or (22):

(21) To the man the woman gave the book.

(22) The woman gave to the man the book.

So this movement test shows that *to the man* is a phrase, because the three words are moved around as a unit. What makes this phrase different from the other phrases we have looked at so far is that it contains the word *to*, a word which belongs to the word class **Preposition** PREPOSITION. Here are some more:

Some English prepositions	on, under, at, of, by, to, about, without

To the man is a preposition phrase, with this internal structure:

(23)

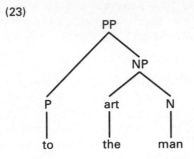

In the three classes of phrase which we have seen so far, the noun, adjective or adverb can be preceded by other things inside the phrase. This is also true of prepositions, which can be preceded by an adverb phrase (24) or a degree modifier (25):

(24)

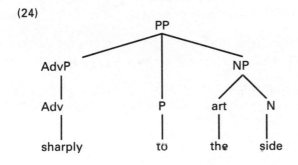

(25)

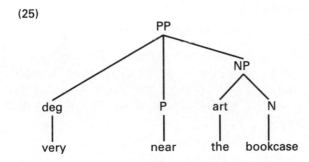

Here are some sentences with preposition phrases in them (italicized), showing some of the positions in which preposition phrases are found:

(26) The ducks all come *from a particular island.*

(27) I stood *by the door* and then I walked *in.*

(28) A picture *of the temple* hung *above the bookcase.*

Is there really a preposition phrase?

In order to explore further the idea of different phrase classes, let's consider what arguments we could make against an alternative claim that there is no preposition phrase, with a preposition instead being like an article or demonstrative – a word class which is found at the beginning of a noun phrase:

(29) (Hypothetical alternative structure for (23))

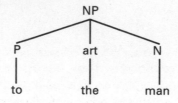

The question is whether this is a better structure than the structure shown in (23). If we apply tests to see whether this is a noun phrase, we find that some tests might suggest that it is; for example, *to the man* can be replaced by a pronoun in some sentences, such as the following:

(30) I gave it *to the man.*

(31) I gave it *him. (acceptable to some speakers)*

But while some tests might suggest that it is a noun phrase, we see that on balance it makes better sense to call it a preposition phrase. Three crucial factors are as follows:

(i) The internal structure of an adjective phrase.
In an adjective phrase, the adjective can sometimes be followed by a noun phrase, but a preposition *always* intervenes (here, *of*):

(32) I am proud of the painting.

(33) *I am proud the painting.

If *of the painting* was a noun phrase just as *the painting* is a noun phrase, then we would not be able to distinguish between the good structure (32) and the bad structure (33). But if we say that *of the painting* is a preposition phrase then we can make a clear distinction:

Generalization

Generalization
Inside an adjective phrase, an adjective cannot be immediately followed by a noun phrase (e.g. (33)) but it can be immediately followed by a preposition phrase (e.g. (32)).

(ii) The degree modifier or adverb which can precede the preposition.
As we saw, a degree modifier or adverb can precede a preposition. If the preposition was simply a word at the beginning of a noun phrase, then we would have to allow a degree modifier or adverb also at the beginning of a noun phrase. That is, instead of (25) we would have:

(34) (Hypothetical alternative structure for (25))

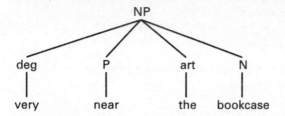

What is wrong with this structure? Specifically, the fact that *very* is there only if the preposition is there; we cannot say *very the bookcase*. This suggests a particular association between the degree modifier *very* and the preposition, which is best captured by putting the preposition in its own preposition phrase, accompanied by the degree modifier.

(iii) A preposition can appear on its own.
One of the characteristics of the head of a phrase is that it can be the only thing in the phrase. A preposition can be on its own, as we see in the following sentence:

(35) I put it down.

Either we would have to interpret *down* as a noun phrase containing only a preposition (a strange result) or we would have to say that *down* is the head of a preposition phrase, and there is nothing else in the phrase. This is the most straightforward result; *down* would then be in a tree structure like this:

(36)   PP

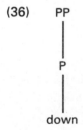

EXERCISES ✎

1. Here are some adverb phrases. Draw tree structures for them. (You will find them progressively more difficult.) The first one is done for you, to illustrate what you should do:

(1) very quickly

Suggested sample answer:

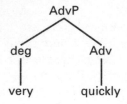

(2) rather slowly

(3) naturally

(4) fortunately for them

(5) rather too quickly

(6) much faster than usual   (*Clue: work out the word class of* usual.)

---

2. Here are some preposition phrases. Draw tree structures for them. (They get progressively harder, and (7) illustrates a structure which we have not seen so far, but which you should be able to work out.)

(1) in the afternoon

(2) on the green table

(3) up a blind alley

(4) completely over the moon

(5) up

(6) right down

(7) out of the side street

---

3. Adverb phrases can appear in various different places in a sentence. Try putting the adverb phrase *unfortunately* into the following sentence in every possible position (you should end up with eight variations).

I chopped the potatoes on the board.

Which positions are unacceptable and why?

---

4. Here are some examples of prepositions on their own in a sentence:

(1) They jumped *down.*

(2) She walked *in.*

(3) We threw it *out.*

Many published grammars of English say that a preposition on its own is not a preposition on its own in a preposition phrase but a different word class called a 'particle'.

Think of two arguments in favour of the alternative idea (presented in this unit) that the word is a preposition in these and similar sentences. (You might find it helpful to think about the tests for phrase class.)

(If you can think of arguments, this exercise illustrates an important point: that the 'grammar' of English is a matter of investigation and argument, not simply a matter of received authority.)

---

5. In the following tree structure diagram, two of the word classes have been left unspecified, and the overall phrase class has been left unspecified.

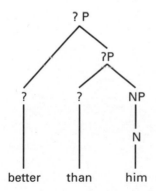

(a) Complete the diagram, replacing all four question marks. (Clue: assume that *than* is the head of the phrase.)

(b) Describe any problems or difficulties which result from your analysis.

---

6. In some languages, prepositions come before a noun phrase, while in others they come *after* a noun phrase. A preposition which comes after a noun phrase is called a POSTPOSITION (you can still use the   **Postposition**

symbol 'P' to stand for postposition, and 'PP' for postposition phrase). Here, for example, is a postposition phrase from Hindi:

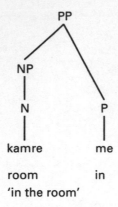

kamre   me

room   in

'in the room'

Look at the corpus languages and work out which languages have prepositions and which have postpositions. Consider particularly the following sentences:

 Chinese: F2, F4
 Madi: F2
 Malay: F5, F6
 Tamil: F1, F2

MORE ON WORD CLASS

4

> The shape of a word (its morphology) can be used as a test for its class. A word class can have sub-classes. Meaning is not a reliable guide to word class. No sentence structure test works perfectly, so it is worth using the results of several tests.

WORD CLASS AND WORD SHAPE

In unit 3 we noted that adverbs have a typical word shape (they often end in *-ly*). This is because adverbs are often constructed by adding the affix *-ly* to an adjective (e.g. the adjective *happy* becomes the adverb *happily*). An AFFIX is a 'piece of word' which (in English) is added at the beginning or end of a word, changing it into a different word. Different affixes attach to different classes of word. Here are some examples:

Affix	What it attaches to	Examples
plural *-s*	attaches only to noun	bag-*s*
comparative *-er*	attaches to adjective (and some adverbs)	small-*er*, fast-*er*
past tense *-ed*	attaches only to verb	walk-*ed*
third person singular *-s*	attaches only to verb	(he) eat-*s*

These affixes do not change the class of the word: a noun *bag* is still a noun when it becomes *bags*. Other affixes do change word class. Here are some examples:

Affix	What it attaches to	What it creates	Examples
-able	verb	adjective	break-*able*, manage-*able*
-ness	adjective	noun	happi-*ness*, sad-*ness*
-ize	noun or adjective	verb	special-*ize*, symbol-*ize*

31

Affixes relate to word class in two ways. An affix at the end of a word can tell you what word class the word is: we can say that some word shapes are associated with particular word classes. And the possibility of adding an affix can tell you whether a word is of a particular class. Consider for example the past tense affix *-ed*, which attaches only to verbs. The following sentence has seven words in it; *-ed* can attach only to *walk*, showing that it is a verb (try adding *-ed* to one of the other six words in sentence (1)!):

(1) I walk to the beach every day.

(2) I walked to the beach every day.

This provides us with another test for word class:

The affix test for word class

THE AFFIX TEST FOR WORD CLASS
The class of a word may be shown by the possibility of attaching a particular affix to it.

The affix test can have some unexpected results. Consider for example the phrase *the poor* in the following sentence:

(3) The poor are starving.

We can see that *the poor* is a noun phrase, because it can be replaced by *they* and begins with an article *the*. We might therefore expect the other word in the phrase, *poor*, to be a noun. But by applying the affix test we can see that it is not. We can add the affix 'superlative *-est*' which attaches only to adjectives, showing that *poor* is actually an adjective:

(4) The poorest are starving.

Thus this is a noun phrase without a noun; an odd structure, which we return to on p. 95.

Morphology

The technical term for 'word shape' is MORPHOLOGY, and from now on we will refer to the morphology of a word rather than the shape of a word. As we will see in the course of this book, the affixes which are part of a word can sometimes be considered as an element of the sentence structure. For example, the English affix 'past tense *-ed*', which we discuss in the next section, conveys crucial information about the time of the events described by the sentence.

VERBS

It is time to introduce the final major word class: the class of verbs.

Some English verbs	kiss, collapse, emphasize, vanish, be, deodorize, break, die, sit, exist, melt, explode, build, expand, vacuum-clean, window-shop, table

The affix test is one of the best tests for an English verb. This is because verbs in English have two special morphological (word shape) characteristics, which no other word class has:

(i) a verb carries the affix -*s* when its subject is third person singular. Since we haven't yet explained what a subject is, we will leave this test for a moment. It basically refers to the fact that the verb *eats* has -*s* because the noun phrase on its left is *he*:

(5) He eats meat.

(ii) a verb can carry the past tense affix -*ed* (or undergo some other morphological change to indicate past tense – as when *eat* changes to *ate*). TENSE is a way of expressing location in time which is specific to verbs. This is perhaps the fundamental difference between (6), with a verb, and (7), with a noun:

Tense

(6) The building collapsed slowly.

(7) The building's slow collapse

(6) tells us something about when the collapse happened – because the verb *collapsed* has past tense. It is possible to add a word like *recent*, which expresses time, to the noun phrase:

(8) The building's recent slow collapse

But while time is now expressed, it is not expressed in the form of tense: there is no morphological change, because there is no verb to change.

Past tense is expressed by a morphological change in the verb. Present tense is typically not overtly expressed (there is no specific present tense affix). But we still say that a verb has present tense, in a sentence like:

(9) They collapse often.

While there is no present tense affix, the 'agreement with the subject' mentioned above happens only when the verb is in present tense – which is an indirect indication of present tense on the verb.

The word class verb is like the word classes noun, adjective, adverb and preposition, in that it is a large word class. But we are assuming a major difference: we have not (at this stage) put the verb into a verb phrase. Instead, we suggest, a verb fits directly into a sentence, like this:

(10)

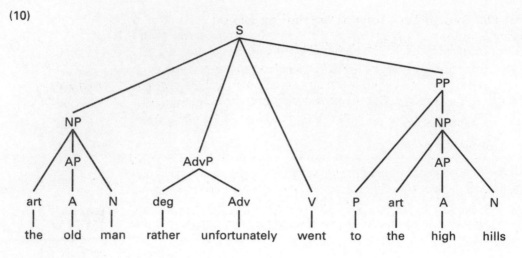

art = article, A = adjective, N = noun, deg = degree modifier, V = verb, P = preposition, AP = adjective phrase, NP = noun phrase, AdvP = adverb phrase, PP = preposition phrase, S = sentence.

This sentence shows all the five main classes of word. Only the verb is not contained in a phrase of its own (i.e. in a verb phrase); instead it is contained in the sentence. It might be helpful to think of the verb as the head of the sentence.

Word sub-classes

By putting a collection of words into a named class, we are saying that all these words have some collection of characteristics in common; for example, they all appear in particular class-specific places in the sentence or phrase. By the same line of reasoning it would be possible to identify some sub-classes *inside* the word classes already identified.

Consider pronouns, for example. We will argue in the next unit that pronouns are nouns (and we have already assumed this in our analyses). However, pronouns are not always found exactly in the same positions as nouns; for example (11) is much more acceptable than (12):

(11) I gave to John the book.

(12) *I gave to John it.

There are other differences, too, which might suggest that pronouns are a sub-class within the larger class of nouns. Exercise 2 in unit 5 gives you the opportunity to examine this further.

A similar problem applies to the auxiliary verbs and the modal verbs. It is possible for a simple sentence to contain *several* verbs. Each of the following examples is a single sentence, but most of these sentences contain more than one verb (all the verbs are italicized):

(13) I *ate* the chocolates.

(14) I *was eating* the chocolates.

(15) I *must eat* the chocolates.

(16) I *could have been eating* the chocolates.

(17) I *have eaten* the chocolates.

Where there are two or more verbs in a single sentence, the final verb is always called the MAIN VERB and can be any one of the thousands of verbs in the language. But the verbs which precede it belong to one of two small groups of verbs; they are either auxiliary verbs or modal verbs.

Main verb

Some English auxiliary verbs	have, be, do
Some English modal verbs	might, may, must, could, can, shall, should, will, would

The MODAL VERBS (abbreviated V_{mod}) express meanings relating to possibility or necessity:

Modal verbs

(18) I might leave.

(19) I should leave.

(20) I must leave.

The AUXILIARY VERBS (abbreviated V_{aux}) differ from main verbs in that they have very specialized meanings or functions. *Have* and *be* can be used to add meanings relating to time, and collaborate to create these meanings with particular affixes on the verb: compare, for example, the different ways in which time is represented in the following sentences, each of which might be describing exactly the same occurrence:

Auxiliary verbs

(21) I broke the window.

(22) I was breaking the window.

(23) I have broken the window.

Do can be added to the beginning of the sentence in a question (see p. 101), or used to support the negation word *not* (see p. 36).

It is easy to distinguish the main verb from auxiliary or modal verbs. In English, the main verb is always the final (rightmost) verb in the sequence; if there is only one verb, it will almost always be the main verb. A complicating fact is that the words *do*, *have* and *be* are ambiguous in that they belong to two classes: there is, for example, an auxiliary version of *have* (expressing time) and a main verb version of *have* (expressing possession):

(24) I have eaten the cake.   **have** *is the auxiliary,* **eaten** *is the main verb*

(25) I have the cake.   *there is no auxiliary,* **have** *is the main verb, expressing possession*

The different versions of *have* fit into different syntactic structures:

(26)

```
                    S
       /      /  |        \
     NP      /   |         NP
      |     /    |        /  \
      N   V_aux  V      art   N
      |    |     |       |    |
      I   have  eaten   the  cake
```

(27)

```
                    S
        /        |        \
      NP         |         NP
       |         |        /  \
       N         V      art   N
       |         |       |    |
       I        have    the  cake
```

Auxiliary verbs and modal verbs can be seen as an example of words which form a sub-class within the wider class of verbs.

NOT

(28) I might not leave.

(29) I have not left.

(30) I did not leave.

(31) *I not left.

(32) *I left not.

As these examples show, *not* appears in a very specific position:

> Generalization
> *Not* appears after the leftmost verb in the sentence, but cannot appear after the rightmost verb in the sentence.

This is why (31) and (32) are both ungrammatical: if there is only one verb, then it is both rightmost *and* leftmost verb, leaving no place for *not* to go. In this case, an extra verb has to be added, the auxiliary verb *do*, to create (30).

Negation

The specific location of *not* means that it belongs to its own class, which we'll call NEGATION (abbreviated as neg). We will put *not* directly into the sentence:

(33)

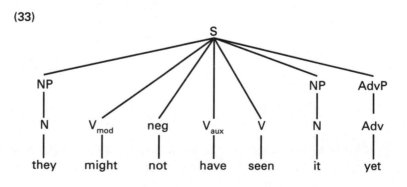

A reason commonly given for putting words into classes is this: we put words into classes in order to indicate that different sorts of words have different sorts of meaning. For example, a preposition often refers to a location in time or place. As we will see, however, meaning does not always match in a clear way with word class. One problem with talking about 'typical meanings' of word classes is that the definitions of word class in terms of meaning are often vague: saying that an adjective is 'a describing word', is unhelpful since more or less any word (including for example the word *lion*, which is a noun) could be called a describing word. Another reason is that traditional meaning-based definitions are sometimes actually wrong: the definition of a verb as 'a doing word' might conceivably include the verb *eat* but it would be hard to claim that the verb *seem* expresses 'doing'. Notice that if you define a verb as a 'doing word' it is also difficult to distinguish the verb *destroy* from the noun *destruction*; in the following examples, both words could be called 'doing words':

(34) They destroy their environment.

(35) Their destruction of their environment.

(As we have seen, the main difference between the verb *destroy* and the noun *destruction* is not in their meaning but in that the verb can carry tense.) A third reason for avoiding meaning-based definitions of word class is that in many cases it can be shown that a particular meaning can be expressed by any one of a number of different word or phrase classes. We will look at two examples of this:

(i) As we have seen, modality (possibility or necessity) can be expressed by a particular word class: verbs, more specifically the sub-class modal verbs:

(36) They might leave. (*possibility*)

(37) They must leave. (*necessity*)

But the same meaning of modality can be expressed by nouns, adjectives and adverbs:

(38) The possibility of their leaving

(39) It's possible that they left.

(40) They possibly left.

Thus modality is a particular kind of meaning, but as we have seen can be expressed by any one of four different classes of word. In this case, word class does not match word function.

(ii) *Near* means more or less the same as *close to*, but they each involve a different word class and different structures. *Near* is a preposition, while *close* is an adjective (in combination with the preposition *to*), giving very different structures for more or less the same meaning:

Word class and meaning

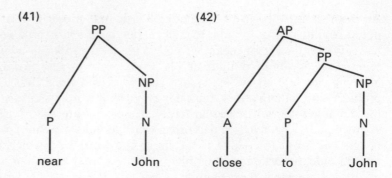

(41)   (42)

PP

P   NP
| |
near   N
|
John

AP

A   PP

P   NP
| |
close to   N
|
John

Why it is difficult to define word classes

On p. 12 we remarked that in introducing word classes such as 'noun', 'adjective' and so on, we did not define them. It should now be clear why. What makes something a noun is that it fits into certain structural locations. This means that the only 'definition' of a noun would be in terms of a set of tests which the noun would have to pass (or pass most of). Where definitions of word class are given in grammars, they are typically based on meaning, since this appears to be an independent fact about a word. But as we have seen, meaning is not a reliable guide to word class, and definitions such as 'a noun is the name of a person, place or thing' have a tendency to collapse when inspected closely.

Using the tests: making a best guess

In this and the previous units we have suggested tests to find out the class of a word, the grouping of words into a phrase, and the class of a phrase. Usually there are several tests which can be tried out for any particular case. This is useful, because few of the tests are watertight. It was suggested once that if a particular word passes some noun tests and some verb tests then it belongs in a kind of half-way class, between noun and verb (the term 'squish' was proposed for this kind of squished-together class). But this kind of approach is not generally taken, partly because it results in a system which gets too complicated. Instead, the usual practice is to make the best guess, based on as many tests as possible. If something looks a bit like a noun and a bit like a verb, then you have to make the choice which seems best justified by the evidence – either noun or verb.

1. The degree modifier *very* can come before an adjective in an adjective phrase. But some adjectives cannot have *very* before them, or sound odd when *very* comes before them. Here are some examples (with adjective phrases italicized):

(1) the *former* president

(2) *the *very former* president

(3) the *buried* treasure

(4) *the *very buried* treasure

(5) *dental* repair

(6) **very dental* repair

Suggest some reasons for the oddness or unacceptability of these adjectives with *very*. (You may decide that they are not in fact adjectives; in this case, you must show what word class they are.)

---

2. This exercise relates to the relation between word class and meaning. A preposition like *after* can express location in time (*after five o'clock*) or location in place (*He ran after the bus*). Can *all* English prepositions do this?

(a) For each of the prepositions below, try to devise two sentences which show it expressing the two kinds of location

(b) Do any of these prepositions appear to have a meaning which does not involve location?

in	on	under
over	before	between
to	at	beneath
for	of	as

---

3. No test works perfectly. For example, while we said that *-able* attaches to verbs, it attaches also to words of another word class.

Give three examples of words which are *not* verbs which the affix *-able* attaches to.

(In order to do this exercise and the next you might find it useful to consult a reverse dictionary or rhyming dictionary, which lists words which *end* in A before words which end in B; hence all *-able* words are grouped together.)

4. This exercise gives you a chance to extend your list of affixes which can prove the class of a word.

(a) Fill in the following table.

(b) If a single affix attaches to several different word classes, you should say that there are different affixes with the same form (for example, there is an *-s* which attaches to nouns and a different *-s* which attaches to verbs).

Affix	Word class it attaches to	Word class it creates	Examples
Affixes at the end of a word ('suffixes')			
-ate			
-ion			
-ment			
Affixes at the beginning of a word ('prefixes')			
under-			
un-			

5. Adverb phrases can appear in the same places, and with more or less the same function as degree modifiers; that is, they indicate the degree of something. For example, the adverb phrases italicized below could be replaced by degree modifiers like *very* (examples (1) and (3)) or *quite* (example (2)).

(1) *intensely* hot

(2) *well* beyond our abilities

(3) *extremely* quickly

Perhaps degree modifiers are a sub-class of adverb (just as pronouns appear to be a kind of noun), which would make the structure of *very hot* as in the diagram below:

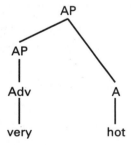

Argue for or against this position, based on what you know about word class (and phrase class).

6. Does *never* belong to the word class 'negation' or 'adverb'?

Answer this question by demonstrating the similarities or differences between *never* and *not*, and between *never* and any word which you know to be an adverb.

---

7. This final exercise asks you to look at the shape of words in some of the languages in the corpus. Word shape or 'morphology' can do very different things in different languages. This exercise may be quite difficult because it asks you to look at new kinds of phenomena, not so far discussed in this book; you should, however, be able to work out some preliminary answers to the questions. Think about the class of words which the affixes are attaching to in each case.

Continue to write word-for-word translations under the sentences in the corpus.

(a) Look at Madi examples N1 and N2. Now, based on example C2, suggest how one might say 'I bought the car (before coming).'

In Tamil, word shape performs a variety of functions, and is much more important than in English. The rest of the questions all relate to Tamil.

(b) Try to describe what the function of the affix *-ai* is. You should be able to do this on the basis of comparing A1, A2 and A3, but you may want to check by looking at other examples.

(c) Both *-ethe* and *-ener* can attach to the word *kondr*. Why is one chosen rather than the other in any particular sentence? Compare, for example, A6 and A7.

(d) Discuss the factors behind the choice of *-naar*, *-nain* and *-nal* in C1–4 (Compare your answer to question (c).)

(e) What is the function of *-aa* in B11? (Compare B1.)

(f) What is the function of *-yum* in K1 and K2?

(g) Tamil allows the words and phrases to come in a wide variety of orders. Suggest how this fact might relate to the importance of word shape in this language – particularly the use of the affix *-ai*?

5 WHERE ENGLISH PHRASES FIT

> Phrases fit directly into a sentence, or fit inside other phrases. All classes of phrase can fit into a sentence. But phrase classes differ in which phrase classes they can fit into.

The following sentence illustrates two different places where a noun phrase can fit.

(1)

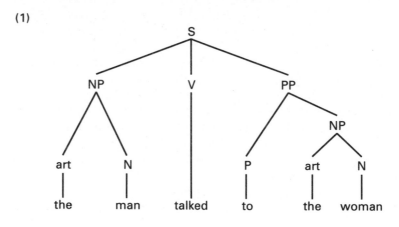

The sentence contains six words and three phrases. But it *immediately* or *directly* contains only one word (the verb *talked*) and two phrases (the noun phrase *the man* and the preposition phrase *to the woman*). This illustrates a simple point about the different places where a phrase can go. The noun phrase *the man* is contained directly in the sentence. But the noun phrase *the woman* is not directly contained by the sentence; instead this noun phrase is directly contained by a preposition phrase. More generally, any class of phrase can fit either directly into a sentence or into another phrase.

Here are some very simple sentences, with their tree structures.
They show some of the cases where different classes of phrase are
contained directly in a sentence.

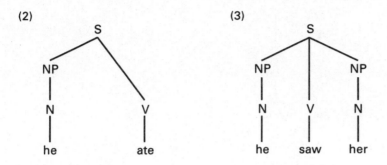

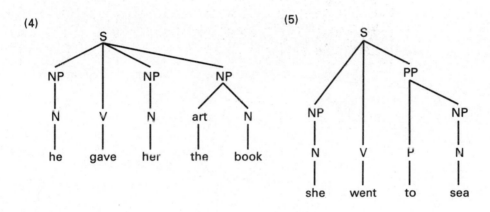

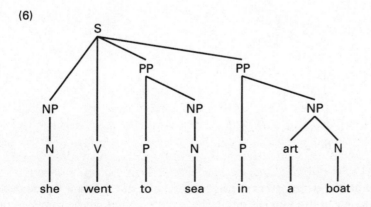

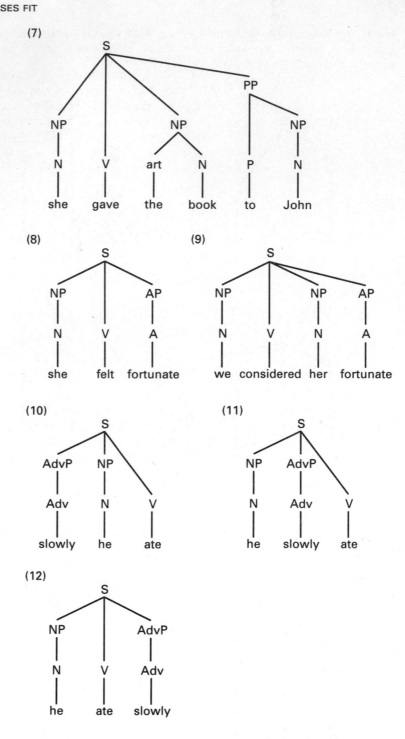

We will now comment further on some of these examples as part of a review of the four different phrase classes and where they fit – both inside sentences, as here, and inside phrases.

There are basically three places where a noun phrase can fit.

(i) A noun phrase can fit directly in a sentence.
In (4), for example, there are three noun phrases all directly contained in the sentence. Noun phrases which are directly contained in the sentence are distinguished from one another by being given different names. One is before the verb: this is the SUBJECT of the verb. Another is after the verb: this is the OBJECT of the verb. In the unusual cases where there is a third noun phrase it is sometimes called the second object of the verb.

**Subject
Object**

He   gave   her   the book.

subject   object   second object

The subject has some special characteristics in English; for example a particular choice of subject can make the verb carry the affix third person singular -*s*:

(13) He eat-*s* cheese.

(ii) A noun phrase can fit directly in a preposition phrase.
We have seen plenty of examples of this; in fact preposition phrases typically contain noun phrases.

(iii) A noun phrase can fit directly into a noun phrase.
Finally, a noun phrase can fit into another noun phrase. The clearest example of this is a 'genitive' noun phrase (which we discuss further on p. 93) – that is, a noun phrase which ends in -*'s* (or a special 'genitive' form of the pronoun such as *his*, *their*, etc.):

(14)   (15)

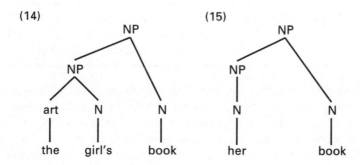

Another way in which a noun phrase can fit into another noun phrase is as in the following structure:

(16)

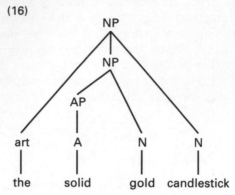

just as nouns can be used as adjectives, so can noun-phrases

solid gold is an adjective phrase, qualifying candle-stick.

Identifying a noun phrase: pronouns as noun phrases

By listing the places where we can find a noun phrase, we provide ourselves with a test for whether something is a noun phrase, based on the position test, repeated here from p. 22.

> THE POSITION TEST FOR PHRASE CLASS
> Each class of phrase appears in certain positions, and not in others.

This is related to another test, repeated here from p. 22:

> THE REPLACEMENT TEST FOR PHRASE CLASS
> A phrase can be replaced by another phrase of the same class.

Pronouns

Consider for example PRONOUNS.

Some English pronouns	I, me, my, you, your, he, him, his, she, her, hers, we, us, our, they, them, their, it, its, himself, each other

rubbish

The fact that pronouns can substitute for noun phrases (e.g. in the replacement test for phrase structure) tells us that they appear in the positions where noun phrases appear. This would suggest that they actually *are* noun phrases. We can illustrate this in detail by considering the fact that a noun phrase can be directly contained in a preposition phrase, noun phrase or sentence; but it *cannot* be directly contained in an adjective phrase. This is what makes (17) unacceptable; *my brother* is directly contained in an adjective phrase:

(17) *I am proud my brother.

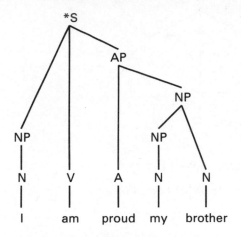

Likewise, it is also not possible to have a pronoun in this position:

(18) *I am proud him.

This suggests that the pronoun is in a noun phrase. Since it is the only occupant of a noun phrase, it is a reasonable assumption that it is the head of the noun phrase – which suggests that it is a noun. So the phrase would have a structure like this:

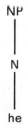

We have been assuming this structure all along (for example in the examples at the beginning of this unit). Now we have justified it. A pronoun is thus a special kind of noun. Notice that we used the head rule for word class (p. 21): the class of a word is the same as the class of its phrase. If the phrase is a noun phrase, its head word is a noun.

It is useful to apply as many tests as possible for anything we want to discover. In exercise 2 we ask you to try some more tests for whether pronouns should be considered as nouns heading noun phrases.

Adjective phrases fit into two basic positions.

WHERE AN ADJECTIVE PHRASE FITS

(i) An adjective phrase can fit directly in a sentence. This is illustrated by examples (8) and (9), and by (19), and by the italicized phrases in (20)–(22).

(19)

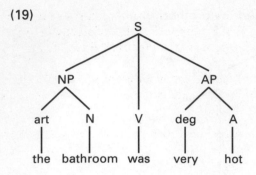

(20) The monster looked *big and green.*

(21) He seems *proud of his children.*

(22) I consider him *happy.*

(ii) An adjective phrase can fit directly into a noun phrase. We have seen plenty of examples of this already.

(23)

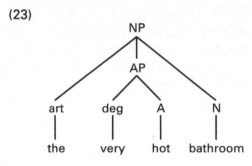

(24) and (25) show further examples; the noun phrase is indicated by putting it in bold type, and the adjective phrase inside it is italicized. (24) shows that two adjective phrases can be found one after another. (25) shows that the adjective phrase can come after the noun.

(24) I saw **a *big green* barn**.

(25) He is **a man *proud of his children***.

Predicative position

Attributive position

The two positions are given different names. Position (i), as in (19), is called the PREDICATIVE POSITION, and the phrase would then be called a predicative adjective phrase. Position (ii), as in (23), is called the ATTRIBUTIVE POSITION and the phrase is called an attributive adjective phrase. In both cases, the adjective phrase characterizes the things described by a noun phrase. In the predicative position, the adjective phrase describes a characteristic (*very hot* in (19)) of something already picked out by the noun phrase (*the bathroom*). In the attributive position, the adjective phrase helps the noun phrase pick something out: *the very hot bathroom* as opposed just to *the bathroom*. Exercise 4 gives you an opportunity to explore some of the differences between adjective phrases in the two positions.

Adjective phrases are the typical examples of phrases which are attributive, but exercise 5 illustrates that other classes of phrase can also appear in this position. Furthermore, other classes of phrase can also appear in predicative position, as exercise 6 illustrates.

Preposition phrases are found in many different places: directly contained in the sentence, and directly contained in all other kinds of phrase. We illustrate this below:

Where a preposition phrase fits

(i) A preposition phrase can be directly contained in the sentence.
This is illustrated by examples (5)–(7).

(ii) A preposition phrase can be directly contained in a noun phrase.

(26)

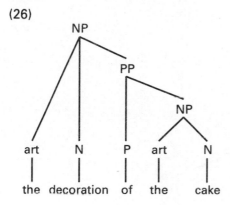

(iii) A preposition phrase can be directly contained in an adjective phrase.

(27)

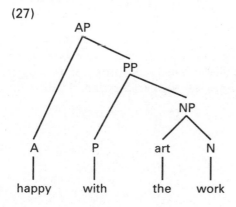

(iv) A preposition phrase can be directly contained in an adverb phrase.

(28)

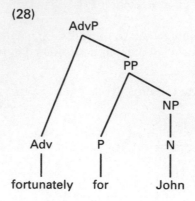

(v) A preposition phrase can be directly contained in a preposition phrase.

(29)

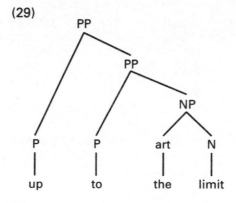

Because preposition phrases can be found in so many different places, it is possible to get quite complex 'stackings' with preposition phrases inside other preposition phrases. Consider, for example, this phrase:

(30) on the table in the office

If this phrase is taken to mean 'on a specific table – the table in the office' then it has a structure like this:

(31)

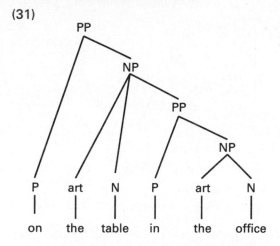

(i) An adverb phrase may fit directly into a sentence. This is illustrated in (10)–(12). As we saw in unit 3 (pp. 23–4 and exercise 3), adverb phrases directly contained in a sentence may appear in many different positions – at the beginning, in the middle or at the end. Adverb phrases are unusual in that they are so 'mobile' in this sense.

Where an adverb phrase fits

(ii) An adverb phrase may fit directly into an adjective phrase.

(32)

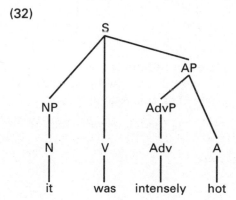

(iii) An adverb phrase may fit directly into an adverb phrase.

(33)

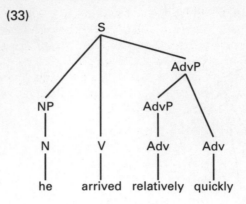

(iv) An adverb phrase may fit directly into a preposition phrase.

(34)

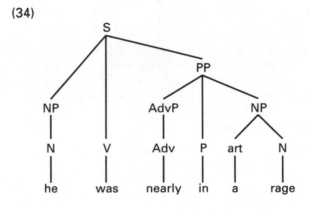

Notice that an adverb phrase cannot fit directly into a noun phrase. Because an adjective phrase *can* fit directly into a noun phrase, this is a useful test for whether something is a noun phrase.

✐ **EXERCISES**

1. You should now be in a position to be able to draw tree structures for whole sentences. This is an essential skill, and will be used increasingly from now on. To give you some practice, draw tree structures for the sentences below; you might notice that many of them fit into exactly the same broad patterns as the sentences illustrated in (2)–(12) at the beginning of this unit. The first one is done for you to show you what an answer should look like.

(1) Dogs particularly dislike black cats.

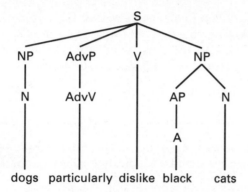

(2) The heron swallowed our fish.

(3) Giant goldfish eat rather quickly.

(4) Black cats bring good luck to the owners.

(5) You seem really sure of yourself.

(6) I gave him five dollars for the book.

(7) He waited for a minute near the station.

---

2. This exercise returns to the question of whether pronouns are nouns heading noun phrases. Find evidence *for* this analysis, and/or *against* this analysis, and come to a conclusion for or against.

You should consider (at least) the following questions:

(a) Can a pronoun appear in every position where a noun phrase appears?
(b) Can a pronoun appear in every position where a noun appears?
(c) Can a pronoun undergo morphological changes which would normally happen to a noun?

3. This exercise asks you to work out the word class of *as*, one of the 'little words' which are found in English (which can be puzzling in terms of their class). Use what you know about word class and phrase class. You may be surprised by the answer which the tests force you to come up with (which must therefore be the right answer).

(a) What is the word class of *as* in the italicized phrase in this sentence?

He was good *as a representative*.

(b) Explain how you know the answer to this question.
(c) In the following italicized phrase, both forms of *as* probably do not belong to the same word class. Explain why, and draw a tree structure to illustrate your answer.

He is *as happy as a lark*.

---

4. In this exercise we explore some of the differences between an attributive adjective phrase and a predicative adjective phrase.

Some adjective phrases can appear only in predicative position (example 1), while others can appear only in attributive position (example 2).

	Predicative position	Attributive position
example 1:	The baby is asleep.	*an asleep baby
example 2:	*The king is future.	the future king

(a) Add three more examples of adjective phrases which can appear only in predicative position.
(b) Add three more examples of adjective phrases which can appear only in attributive position.
(c) Try to explain why these particular adjectives are restricted in this way.

Some adjectives can appear in both positions but with different sorts of meaning.

A	B
Attributive position	Predicative position
(3) He is a beautiful swimmer.	The swimmer is beautiful.
(4) This is a clever dog.	This dog is clever.
(5) This is an enormous pea.	This pea is enormous.

(d) Compare the A and B sentences and discuss the potential differences in meaning.

5. This exercise shows that phrases other than the adjective phrase can be in attributive position.

    (1) the country inn

    (2) a sister ship

    (3) the happy sailor

    (4) the down escalator

The phrases in (1)–(4) fit into the structure indicated here, where a phrase is in attributive position:

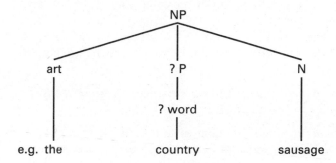

    (a) Prove the class of phrase and class of word in each case.

The noun phrase in (5) is unacceptable – it is supposed to mean 'a ship which is sister to the USS Enterprise'; compare it with the acceptable (6) and (7):

    (5) *a sister to the USS Enterprise ship

    (6) a ship, sister to the USS Enterprise

    (7) a sister ship

    (b) Formulate a generalization which explains why noun phrases like (5), (8) and (9) are ungrammatical.

    (8) *the happy with his life sailor

    (9) *the up the outside escalator

---

6. This exercise shows that phrases other than the adjective phrase can appear in the predicative position.

    (1) He seems *somewhat foolish*.

    (2) He seems *a bit of a fool*.

    (3) He seems *in a bit of a mess*.

    (a) The italicized phrases in (1)–(3) are all in predicative position. Prove the phrase class of each phrase.

(b) Adverb phrases do not appear in predicative position. Explain why.

---

7. We conclude with an exercise which uses the corpus. This exercise may be quite difficult, in part because it introduces some phenomena which do not exist in English.

Examine the Malay sentences F1–6, and consider the word *ada* which appears in F1–4.

(a) Does *ada* belong to the same word class in all four examples?
(b) Does *ada* always function in the same way or always have the same meaning?
(c) Draw tree structures for Malay sentences F1, F3 and F4. (Assume that *disana* in F3 is an adverb in an adverb phrase.)

Now examine the Cantonese Chinese sentences F1-6 and consider the word *hai*.

(d) Does *hai* belong to the same word class in all examples?
(e) Does *hai* always function in the same way or have the same meaning?
(f) Draw tree structures for sentences F1, F4–6.

DRAWING TREE STRUCTURES FOR SIMPLE SENTENCES

6

Tree structures are governed by certain conventions, which relate to particular conceptions of sentence structure. There are similarities in word or phrase order between different classes of constituent in a language. Languages differ in the word classes which they use.

In this unit we reflect on the structure of simple sentences. We suggest some guidelines for drawing tree structures, and look at some of the differences in sentence structure which exist between different languages.

A tree structure is a way of illustrating the structure of a sentence or phrase. However, there are certain rules about drawing tree structures, which have been implicit in the tree structures drawn so far. These rules are based on certain ideas about *what kind of structure* sentences have. We look at these ideas in turn. In order to discuss tree structures we need to distinguish three basic components: lines, nodes and labels, as illustrated in (1). 'Line' is self-explanatory. A NODE is where a line starts or ends (often several lines start or end at the same node). A label is the name of a phrase or word class, and is attached to a node. In the diagram below we have left one node unlabelled (normally we write the label in place of the node).

FOUR RULES ABOUT TREE STRUCTURES

Node

(1)

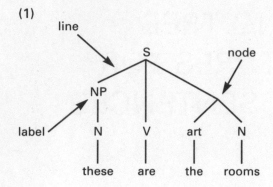

We now look at the four rules about tree structures.

(i) *No horizontal lines* The lines have a simple function: to show that one node contains another. In (1) S contains NP, NP contains N, and N contains the word *these*. The convention is that the node which contains is above the node which is contained – hence the lines joining them must never be horizontal (such a line would be meaningless).

(ii) *Every node is labelled* Each node stands for a constituent of the sentence – a word, phrase, or (the topmost node) the sentence itself. Since every word or phrase belongs to a class, every node must have a label to show the class of the word or phrase.

(iii) *Lines do not cross* This rule depends on a particular view of sentence structure, and not everyone agrees with it (some linguists allow crossing lines). The view that lines should not cross means that phrases and words do not overlap. We can illustrate the issue with an interesting example, the so-called 'phrasal verb'. A PHRASAL VERB is a verb which is associated with a preposition phrase headed by a particular preposition; often the preposition is the only thing in the phrase (and so is called a 'particle' in some grammars, see p. 29). Consider, for example, the combination of *throw* and *up*, which together mean 'vomit', as in the following sentences:

Phrasal verb

(2) I threw up my dinner.

(3) I threw my dinner up.

A standard analysis (along the lines outlined in this book) would be these tree structures:

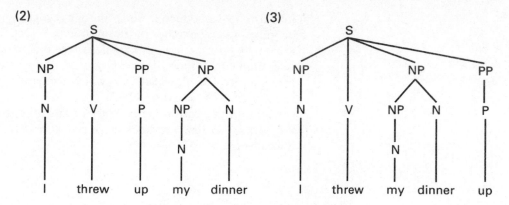

(2)   (3)

However, since *throw* and *up* combine to create a single meaning, it might be argued that they should form a single constituent of some kind. Such an argument would be based on the assumption that sentence structure mirrors the meaning of the sentence – an assumption we do *not* make in this book. On such an assumption, however, it might be argued that lines should cross in the tree structure for (3):

(3a) Alternative structure

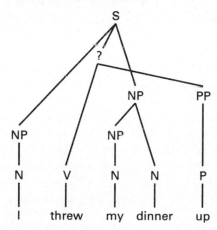

We do not recommend such an analysis, though we recognize that it is a possible one. It raises a number of problems which would have to be solved – such as the class of the node labelled '?'. Since we do not assume that the sentence structure directly reflects the meaning of the sentence, we have no need for such an analysis, and suggest that lines should never cross.

(iv) *A node is joined to only one node above it (i.e. is contained by only one node)* This rule is based on the related ideas that the tree diagram indicates containment and that phrases do not overlap. Each node in the tree should be joined to just one higher node, though a higher node can be joined to any number of lower nodes. We can illustrate this rule by presenting an example where it is broken (this rule, unlike the others, can be broken in some cases). This example involves the word *not*, which sometimes appears in a sentence not as a distinct word but as an affix on another word. In this case it is necessary to have the tree structure drawn so that the lines converge downwards rather than diverge:

(4)

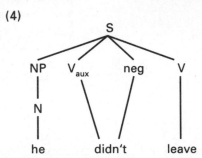

Here, the node which is the word *didn't* is joined to two nodes above it, and is contained by two nodes, thus breaking the general rule. This kind of tree structure will result when parts of a word have an independent role in sentence structure.

Word and phrase order revisited
Open class
Closed class

The word classes can be divided into two groups, depending on how easy it is to add new words. If it is easy to add words to a class, it is called an OPEN CLASS, and if it is hard (i.e. happens rarely) it is called a CLOSED CLASS. For example, it is only very occasionally that a new pronoun or quantifier is added to a language, while new nouns are added almost daily. We have included some sub-classes (the sub-class of auxiliary verbs is a closed class, even though it belongs to the open class of verbs).

Open classes	*Closed classes*
noun, verb, adjective, adverb	preposition, article, demonstrative, quantifier, numeral, degree modifier, negation, auxiliary verb, modal verb, pronoun

Some of the closed class words head phrases: this is true at least of prepositions and pronouns. But notice where the others are found:

article, demonstrative, quantifier, numeral: precede the noun which is the head of the noun phrase.
degree modifier: precedes the adverb which is the head of the adverb phrase, the adjective which is the head of the adjective phrase, the preposition which is the head of the preposition phrase.

negation, *auxiliary verb*, *modal verb*: precede the verb which can
be thought of as the head of the sentence.

The generalization is simple:

> In English, a closed class item precedes the head of the phrase
> or sentence.

Unless, of course, it *is* the head of the phrase, as in the case of prepositions and pronouns.

This generalization is interesting because it proposes that the order of constituents can be generalized across different classes of phrase, and suggests that phrases are like sentences in certain ways. There are other similarities. For example, the order of subject, verb and object in a sentence like (5) can be repeated in the order of noun phrase, noun, and preposition phrase in a noun phrase like (6):

(5) I   read   the book.

(6) My   reading   of the book

Another similarity, which is found in many languages, involves the order of the verb and the object, compared to the order of the preposition and the noun phrase which accompanies it. Typically, if the verb comes before the object, the language has prepositions (P – NP order); while if the verb comes after the object (e.g. at the end of the sentence) the language has postpositions (NP – P order). Exercise 8 gives you a chance to check this for the languages in the corpus (this cross-linguistic generalization doesn't always work, incidentally).

We will now suggest some guidelines and shortcuts for drawing tree structures. We give some further guidelines in later units (for example, p. 77, when we look at subordinate clauses). In order to draw a tree structure for a sentence, there are basically five things you need to do. They are listed below, together with some suggestions as to how to do each one. It is important to remember, though, that there is no particular order in which they should be done, and that they interact with each other. Sometimes it is easier to begin by determining word class, but you might first have to determine phrase grouping and phrase class before it is possible to identify word class. The tests referred to are summarized on p. 137.

Guidelines for drawing tree structures

(i) Determine the word class of each word.
Some tests you can use include: affix test for word class, the head rule and the internal structure test for phrase class (a word may appear in a typical position inside a phrase).

(ii) Determine how words group into phrases.
Some tests you can use include: the replacement test and the movement test. Any closed class words should be at the beginning of a phrase. Any open class words will each head their own phrase.

(iii) Determine how words and phrases combine into larger phrases.
Use the same tests as you used for (ii). Use also your knowledge of phrase structures (unit 5).

(iv) Determine the phrase class of each phrase.
Some tests you can use include: the position test, replacement test and internal structure test for phrase class.

(v) Determine how words and phrases combine into the sentence.
Use your knowledge of sentence structure (unit 5). You know that the verb is directly contained in the sentence; you would expect there to be a subject on the left of the verb, usually a noun phrase. There might be another noun phrase or two after the verb, followed perhaps by preposition phrases. Adverb phrases might appear in any position.

A worked example

To illustrate these procedures, we will work out a tree structure for this sentence:

(7) They are examples of the very austere style of the period.

Some of the words are instantly identifiable because they belong to closed classes. *They* is a noun, *of* is a preposition, *the* is an article, and *very* a degree modifier. So we can begin to construct a tree:

The degree modifier *very* usually comes before an adverb or adjective in an appropriate type of phrase; *austere* is a candidate – and we can see that *very austere* is a phrase by movement (*the style was very austere*). So we can add this to our diagram. A noun and an article are found only in a noun phrase, so we can add these to the diagram:

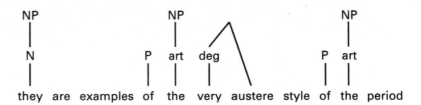

The second noun phrase has an article but no noun; an appropriate noun might be *style* (check with the affix test: it can be pluralized . . . *styles of the period*). This suggests that *very austere* must be an adjective phrase because it is between an article and a noun, and by the head rule *austere* is an adjective. The third noun phrase has an article but no noun. *Period* is the only available word, and we can confirm that it is a noun by pluralizing it. So we now have the following:

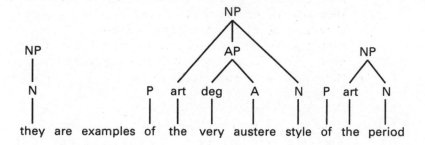

A preposition is often followed by a noun phrase, so we can hypothetically join these up. *Examples* is clearly a noun because it is plural. And *are* must be a main verb (rather than an auxiliary, because it is the only verb in the sentence). Once we add this we can draw in the sentence, and connect the verb and the first NP – the subject – to it.

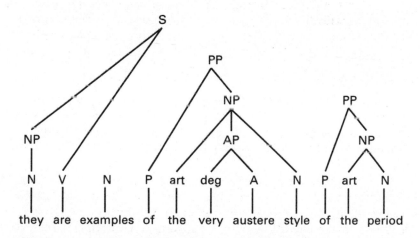

Now let's try connecting it all together. It is possible to show that *examples of the very austere style of the period* is a single phrase, by movement: *examples of the very austere style of the period is what they are*. It is also possible to show that *the very austere style of the period* is a phrase – and more specifically a noun phrase, by substitution: *they are examples of this*, or by movement: *the very austere style of the period is what they are examples of*. This suggests a phrase-inside-phrase structure like this:

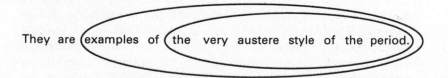

Which represents a tree structure like this:

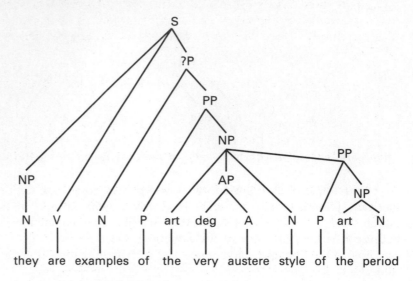

Finally, we can identify the missing phrase node ?P as a noun phrase, by the internal structure test – it contains a noun *examples* (affix test: it is plural) followed by a preposition phrase – a typical noun phrase structure.

Why is an adjective always in an adjective phrase?

We have said that an open class item is always contained in its own phrase. This means that if you have a sequence like (8), the adjective must be in an adjective phrase as in (9), and not just directly contained in the noun phrase, as in (10):

(8) the happy man

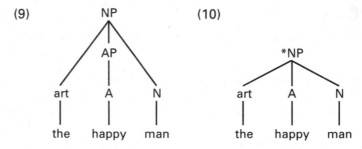

Why is (9) preferred over (10)? One reason is to simplify the description of sentence structure. The argument goes like this: we know that an adjective phrase can come between an article and a noun ('generalization A'), because of examples like *the very happy man*, so we know that the structure in (9) is possible. We also know that an adjective phrase can contain just an adjective ('generalization B'), again making the structure in (9) possible. There is no need to invent a third generalization ('generalization C') which would say that an *adjective* can come between an article and a noun. If we can get by with two generalizations, we need not invent a third. There is more to be said about this, but like other questions in this unit it borders on linguistic theory and takes us beyond the concerns of this book. We recommend, therefore, that for now you choose (9) instead of (10).

Languages differ in what classes their words fit into. Here are some examples:

Other word classes in other languages

(i) Every language has nouns and verbs, but in some languages there are, for example, no adjectives, and the role that English adjectives play is played instead by nouns or verbs.

(ii) Prepositions do not exist in all languages; exercise 5 illustrates some of the ways that the Fon language expresses the 'location' meanings expressed by English prepositions.

(iii) In English, tense is expressed by an affix on the verb, but in some languages there is a closed class of words which express tense. Cantonese Chinese, for example, has a word *choa* which can be used to express past tense (it comes after the verb).

(iv) Both Chinese and Malay have a closed class of words called a 'classifier' (cl.). It can be illustrated using Chinese examples from the corpus.

(A5) yu   sik   choa   kó   chaet   kai
fish   eat   past   that   cl.   chicken
'A fish ate that chicken.'

(D6) ngo   taido   kó   kò   yan
I   saw   that   cl.   man
'I saw that man.'

The demonstrative 'that' is translated by a demonstrative word *kó* followed by a classifier; the classifier which follows depends on the meaning of the noun. If the noun is *kai* ('chicken'), the classifier is *chaet*; if the noun is *yan* ('man'), the classifier is *kò*. The classifier thus relates to the classification of nouns (hence its name). The use of classifiers resembles the use of gender in a language like French or German. Again, nouns are classified and, depending on their classification, there might be changes in other words – such as the definite article; in French, the definite article is *le* if the noun is classified as 'masculine' and *la* if the noun is classified as 'feminine'.

EXERCISES ✎

It is essential at this stage that you should be able to do exercise 1. You may find that the other exercises in this unit are quite hard (particularly 3 and 5); they are designed to push you and extend your thinking about sentence structure.

1. Draw tree structures for the following English sentences:

(1) These people here have a special relationship with wild animals.

(2) The completion of this form is exceptionally important.

(3) You should answer each question fully.

(4) A reasonably effective approach means at least a chance of success.

2. What is unusual from a structural point of view about the degree modifier *enough*?

3. The following words often appear on their own, though they can also appear inside a sentence.

yes
please
thanks
oh
goodbye

For each word:

(a) Discuss whether it belongs to a word class. (All words discussed in this book so far *do* belong to a word class; but perhaps some English words do not. In order to discuss this, you will need to consider again the purpose of putting a word into a class.)

(b) If it belongs to a word class, prove which one it belongs to (invent new classes if necessary).

4. The following sentences in Arabic show some interesting differences from equivalent English sentences.

(1) aT-Taqsu   jamiilun
the-weather   nice
'The weather is nice.'

(2) kaana   aT-Taqsu   jamilan
    was   the-weather   nice
    'The weather was nice.'

(3) al-mudarrisu   fii   aS-Saffi
    the-teacher   in   the-class
    'The teacher is in the class.'

(4) sawfa   yakuunu al-mudarrisu fii aS-Saffi ba'ada sa'a-tin
    (future) be   the-teacher in the class after hour-one
    'The teacher will be in the class after one hour.'

(a) What are the differences in word order between equivalent English and Arabic sentences and phrases?

(b) What other kind of difference between English and Arabic do examples (1) and (3) demonstrate? Describe the difference as precisely as you can.

(c) Draw tree structure diagrams for all four sentences. (You may decide that some of the verbs are auxiliary verbs: the crucial question is whether the verb can be alone in a sentence – if it can, then it is a main rather than an auxiliary verb.)

(This exercise is continued in unit 7, exercise 4.)

---

5. Location is often expressed by prepositions in English. But some languages, such as the West African language Fon typically use other word classes to express location.

(a) Look at examples (1)–(3). What word class expresses the meaning of 'to' in Fon?

(1) koku   so   ason
     Koku   took   crab
     'Koku took a crab.' (*Koku is a name*)

(2) koku   yi   axi
     Koku   go   market
     'Koku went to market.'

(3) koku   so   ason   yi   axi
     Koku   take   crab   go   market
     'Koku took a crab to the market' (i.e. took in a direction away from the speaker).

(b) On the basis of (4), make a guess at the Fon translation of 'Koku came to the market.'

(4) koku so ason wa axi

'Koku brought a crab to the market' (i.e. brought in a direction towards the speaker).

Look at the phrases in (5)–(8). The Fon word *me* is found in three examples; it is the same word, belonging to the same class in all three. The classes of the other words are: *o* = article, *xo* = noun, *dan* = noun (*dan* is a person's name).

(5) me   o

inside   the

'the inside'

(6) xo   o   me

belly   the   in

'in the belly'

(7) dan   xo

Dan's   belly

'Dan's belly'

(8) dan   xo   me

Dan's   belly   in

'in Dan's belly'

(c) What is the word class of *me*?

(d) Draw tree structures for the four phrases.

(Incidentally, (8) is the word 'Dahomey', the name of the kingdom where Fon was spoken before colonial divisions of West Africa.)

---

6. For each language in the corpus describe the order and position in the sentence of: negation, auxiliary and modal verbs and the main verb. (You do not need to restrict yourself to looking at sections G and H, though these are the most relevant.)

---

7. Draw tree structures for the following simple sentences from the corpus. (Continue to add word-for-word translations under the sentences in the corpus as you do so.)

For example, the first Chinese example would have this tree structure:

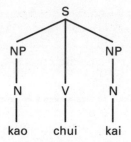

kao chui kai

Chinese A1, B1, D8, H1

Madi: A1, A5, D2, F1, H1 (Note: you will have to make a decision on the word class of *ra*; make a best guess if you have to. If you are unsure about *not*, look at M1 in comparison with H2.)

Malay: A1, D1, D10, F6, H3 (Note: you will have to decide what *telah* is; try comparing the B sentences with each other.)

Tamil: A1, D8, F1, H1

---

8. For each language in the corpus, work out the order of grammatical words, head and other phrases in:

  (a) the sentence (here, you may find that order is not fixed, or is only partly fixed);

  (b) the adjective phrase;

  (c) the noun phrase;

  (d) the preposition phrase (consult your answers to exercise 6 in unit 3, pp. 29–30).

  (e) Now, for each language find out whether there is any consistency of order between the different kinds of phrase and the sentence.

For example, this is what you might do with Chinese:

  (a) *the sentence appears to have a basic 'subject – auxiliary – verb – object' order (S V_{aux} V O), illustrated, for example, by G3.*

  (b) *the adjective phrase has an order 'deg – A', illustrated by D8.*

On the basis of just these two, we could say that there seems to be a consistent ordering of closed class word before the head (as in English, in fact). In order to complete this analysis of Chinese we would now look at noun phrase and preposition phrase.

---

9.   (a) In what circumstances is a classifier used to accompany a noun in Chinese? (It is found after the word meaning 'that'; is it found after other demonstratives? Where else is it found?)

(b) Malay has the word class 'classifier'. Give some examples of classifiers in Malay, by comparing examples D4 and D6–9. (Note: *yang* is not a classifier.)

(c) Are there any words in English which function like classifiers?

SENTENCES WHICH ARE CONTAINED IN SENTENCES AND PHRASES

7

> A sentence can be contained in another sentence or inside a phrase. This kind of contained sentence, called a subordinate clause may be introduced by various types of constituent. Subordinate clauses may differ from non-subordinate sentences in their internal structure.

Up to now we have looked at sentences which are 'simple' in a specific way: they did not *contain* any other sentences. In this unit we look at more complex sentences, which contain other sentences either directly as in (1), or indirectly as in (2).

(1)

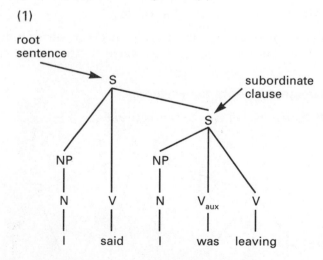

(2)

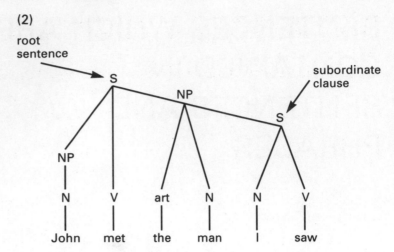

Subordinate clause
Root sentence

When a sentence is contained it is called a SUBORDINATE CLAUSE. When a sentence is not contained it is called a ROOT SENTENCE. The subordinate clause always appears lower in the tree than the root sentence. Notice that we use the same class label 'S' for both types of sentence.

Where sub-ordinate clauses are found

Subordinate clauses can appear in many of the places where phrases can appear, and can play similar roles to those phrases. For example, a sentence (italicized) can be the object of a verb (as in (3) and (4)), or its subject (as in (5)).

(3) I said *that I was leaving*.

(4) We all told him *that it was useless*.

(5) *Whether he has gone* is a mystery.

A subordinate clause can be like an adverb phrase in expressing the circumstances of an event, such as when or where something happened:

(6) We ate *where we ate yesterday*.

(7) *Because he left* we sighed with relief.

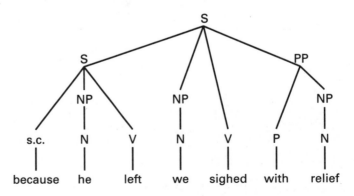

In the cases discussed so far, the subordinate clause is directly contained in another sentence. However, a sentence may also be contained inside a phrase:

(8) the belief *that the earth is flat*   sentence is contained in an NP

(9) proud *to be a human being*   sentence is contained in an AP

(10) after *I left*   sentence is contained in a PP

In English, there are several differences between a root sentence and a subordinate clause.

Differences between root and subordinate clauses

(i) A subordinate clause can start with a word or phrase or combination which indicates that it is subordinate, such as the word *that* in (11):

(11) I said ***that** he was leaving*.

(ii) A subordinate clause can be infinitive as in (12), using the infinitive marker *to*.

(12) I wanted ***to** leave*.

The word *to* can of course be a preposition. But here we have a different word belonging to a different word class. We will call *to* an INFINITIVE MARKER, 'inf' for short.

Infinitive marker

(iii) A subordinate clause can have *me* as the subject; a root clause can have only *I*. The same pattern holds for *her* vs. *she*, *us* vs. *we*, etc. (this relates to the distinction between 'accusative' and 'nominative' case which we return to briefly on p. 104):

(13) He wanted ***me** to leave*.

(14) *Me wanted to leave.

A subordinate clause can be introduced by a word or combination of words which indicates that it is subordinated. Sometimes this is done by a word of the closed grammatical word class SUBORDINATING CONJUNCTION.

Constituents which subordinate the clause

Subordinating conjunction

Some English subordinating conjunctions	that, whether, because, if, how

A subordinating conjunction is put at the beginning of the subordinate clause, as in the following examples ('s.c.' stands for subordinating conjunction in the tree structure).

(15) I left ***because** I wanted to catch the train*.

(16) I asked **whether** *John was leaving.*

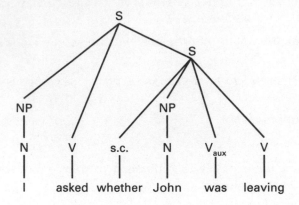

Instead of using a subordinating conjunction, a 'question phrase' like *when* can be put at the beginning of the subordinate clause (a question phrase is a noun phrase, adjective phrase, etc., modified for questions, as we discuss in unit 10).

(17) **When** *we arrived* the party began.

(18) **How difficult** *this is going to be* depends on you.

(19) I asked **whose book** *this was.*

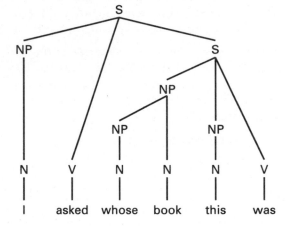

The subordinating words or phrases we have looked at so far are all inside and at the front of the subordinate clause. But it is also possible to use a preposition, outside the sentence, to subordinate the sentence:

(20) **After** *we left,* the cat died.

(21) **By** *reading the book* we managed to understand better.

(22) **As** *you said,* . . .

These constructions are built like this (i.e. the sentence is contained in a PP):

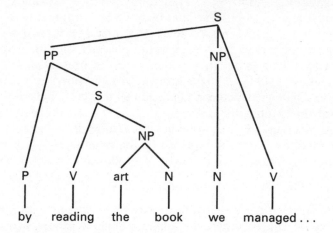

It is possible to combine a preposition outside the sentence with a subordinating conjunction *inside* the sentence:

(23) ***In that*** *we are new here*, we feel embarrassed.

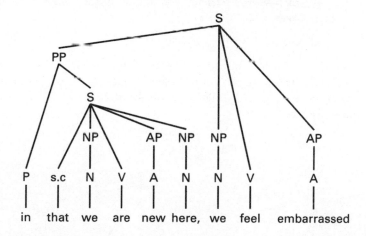

Finally, we'll let *you* work out what the (rather complex) structure of the following subordinating construction is. Draw a tree structure for the following sentence:

(24) I left *in order to catch the train*.

We have not yet addressed the question of how we can identify a group of words and phrases as a sentence. The same tests are in principle available here as are used to identify a phrase as being of a particular class. There are essentially two kinds of test: what the internal structure looks like (including its head), and where the constituent is (replacement and position).

Identifying constituency and class for a sentence

There are certain things which are found only directly contained in a sentence; these are all clues to the presence of a sentence. They include subordinating conjunction, infinitive, auxiliary verb and modal verb. It is possible that main verbs are found elsewhere than directly contained in a sentence (see unit 11), though we have not argued for this yet; in any case, the presence of a main verb should not be taken as reliable evidence of the presence of a sentence, though it could be taken into account as possible evidence. If a subordinate sentence contains one of these closed class items, it can easily be identified as a sentence. However, not every sentence does, and in this case it is possible to appeal to position or replacement. A sentence can often be replaced by the noun phrase *it* or by another sentence. Consider, in this light, the following italicized constituent:

(25) I saw *them running*.

The fact that it is possible to replace *them running* with *it* or another sentence, suggests that *them running* might be a sentence:

(26) I saw it.

(27) I saw that they were running.

Tests can also be used to identify the boundaries of an embedded clause – which words/phrases are in the clause and which are not. Consider (28):

(28) I want him to leave.

The presence of *to* indicates that *to leave* is part of a subordinate clause. But is *him* in the subordinate clause (Structure A) or the root sentence (Structure B)? This is a question about the constituency of the sentence.

Structure A

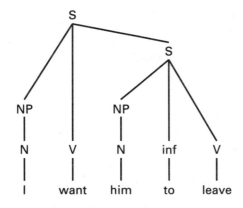

Structure B

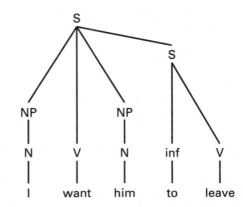

By replacement we can answer this question. A sentence can often be replaced by the noun phrase *it* or by another sentence. In this case, it is structure B which is indicated by the tests, shown in (29) and (30); *to leave* cannot be replaced on its own (hence the ungrammaticality of (31) and (32).)

(29)   I want *for him to leave*.

(30)   I want *it*.

(31) * I want him *for him to leave*.

(32) * I want him *it*.

Where several sentences are combined, it can sometimes be tricky to work out which sentences are subordinate clauses. In this section, we suggest some strategies for solving this problem. The first strategy builds on the following assumption:

Strategies for deciding which sentences are subordinate

> There is only one main verb in a sentence or clause (there can also be auxiliary or modal verbs, accompanying that verb).

So start by counting main verbs (ignore any auxiliary or modal verbs). Each main verb is in a separate sentence. For example, sentence (33) has three main verbs (italicized). One will be the verb which heads the root sentence. The other two can only head subordinate clauses.

(33) I *suggested* to her that they might *want* to *leave*.

We now need to distinguish the verbs which head the subordinate clauses from the verb which heads the root sentence. The following generalizations can guide us:

> If a verb is infinitive, it heads a subordinate clause.

> If a verb has *me*, *him*, *her*, *us* or *them* as a subject, it heads a subordinate clause.

This means that in (33) *leave* heads a subordinate clause. Another clue involves subordinating conjunctions.

> The first main verb after a subordinating conjunction heads a subordinate clause.

So this means that in (33) *want* heads a subordinate clause. By elimination, this means that *suggested* heads the root clause. Now try putting the sentences together around each verb. *I* is the subject of *suggested*, and *to her* is its object. *That* must be at the beginning of a subordinate clause, which has *want* as its head; so *they*, since it is between these words, must be the subject. *To* belongs in another subordinate clause, with the verb *leave*. This gives us an almost complete picture of the sentence like this:

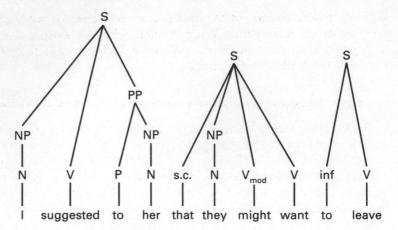

We have put the root sentence node higher than the two subordinate sentence nodes, as is always the case. But we have not worked out how the three sentences fit together. We can now use our tests for phrase structure, which will work equally well for subordinate clauses. The word *it* can replace a sentence. We find that it replaces *that they might want to leave*, suggesting that this is a single constituent:

(34) I suggested it to her.

We can also move *that they might want to leave*, again suggesting that it is a constituent:

(35) That they might want to leave I suggested to her.

So this means that the two subordinate sentences are combined into a single constituent. In fact, the way they are combined is like this:

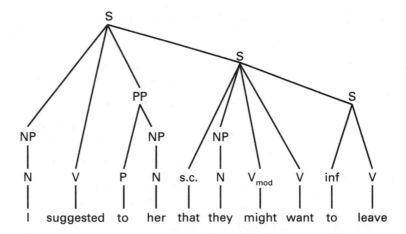

The crucial claim is that *to leave* is subordinated under *want*. We can reach this conclusion by looking at the meaning of the sentence. *To leave* is what is 'wanted', meaning that *to leave* is the object of *want*, and hence subordinated under it. Notice that this method – considering the meaning of the sentence – can also be used to decide that *that*

they might want to leave is subordinated as the object of *suggested*. Here, as always, it is worth using any strategy which gets you to a tree structure (though it is usually worth using several strategies, to make sure that you get to the right result).

✐ **EXERCISES**

1. This activity is intended to give you practice in working out which sentences are subordinate and which one is the root. For each sentence below, draw a cut-down tree structure along the lines illustrated, where each verb is joined to a separate S, and the S nodes are then put under each other to show which sentences are subordinate to which others. The first one is done for you.

(1) When he arrives I might ask her to show him the book.

Sample answer for sentence (1):

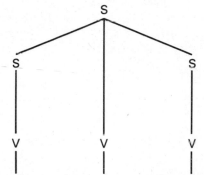

when he arrives I might ask her to show him the book

(2) Where I was a student no one ever wanted to watch films.

(3) They never decided whether to ask him to be their leader.

(4) I know that she knows that it is not true.

(5) If he wants to, he can come and tell us his story.

---

2. A subordinate clause need not have a subject; we can see this by comparing tensed (1) and tenseless (2) subordinated sentences:

(1) John told Peter that he should leave.

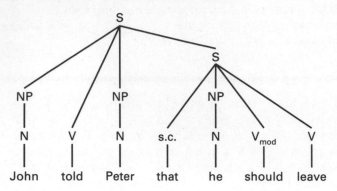

(2) John told Peter to leave.

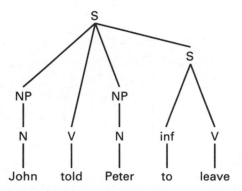

The sentence *to leave* does not have a subject, but we have to some-how decide what the sentence means – that is, who the person is who is leaving. In this sentence, it is the object in the root sentence which stands for the missing subject of the subordinated sentence; *Peter* is interpreted as the person who is to leave. This process is called CONTROL: *Peter* controls the subordinate (missing) subject.

Control

(a) Justify the claim that *Peter* is the object of *told* in (2).
(b) For each sentence below, describe whether it is the subject or the object of the root sentence which controls the missing subject in the subordinate clause (e.g. in (3) the root subject controls the subordinate subject).

(3) Rick wanted to leave early.

(4) Rick told Alice to leave early.

(5) Betty asked to leave early.

(6) Betty asked Val to leave early.

(7) Val and Rick both decided to leave early.

(c) On the basis of (2)–(7), try to make a generalization about which noun phrase in a root sentence typically controls a subject in a subordinate clause.

(d) The following sentence is accepted by some English speakers, with the interpretation given:

(8) John promised Mary to give her the book

(*interpreted as meaning that John will give her the book*)

You should find that this sentence does not fit with your generalization. Explain what is unusual about it.
(Some English speakers do not accept this sentence, and consider it to be uninterpretable; this may be related to its unusual nature.)

(e) *Him* can refer to *John* in (9) but not in (10). Try to explain why.

(9) John persuaded Mary to send him the book

(10) John promised Mary to send him the book.

---

3. Draw tree structures for the following sentences (draw complete tree structures, with all nodes labelled).

(1) I wanted to ask whether it was true.

(2) There was a suggestion that the monkeys might be in danger.

(3) Fairly soon we expect Mary to ask us to leave.

(4) That young man can't decide whether to become a fireman.

---

4. This is a continuation of unit 6, exercise 4.

(d) Consider the following English sentences:

(1) I consider the weather nice.

(2) I heard the teacher in the class.

Provide an argument that *the weather nice* and *the teacher in the class* are a kind of sentence. (Try replacement.)

(e) Compare the English sentences (1) and (2) with the Arabic sentences (3) and (4) below. Comment on the similarities and differences between English and Arabic which this comparison reveals.

(3) aT-Taqsu   jamiilun
    the-weather   nice
    'the weather is nice.'

(4) al-mudarrisu fii   aS-Saffi
     the-teacher   in   the-class
     'the teacher is in the class.'

---

5. Draw tree structures for the following sentences from the corpus (all of which involve subordinate clauses):

Chinese: J1, J2
Madi: J1, J3
Malay: J1, J2
Tamil: J2, J3

COORDINATION, APPOSITION AND COMPOUNDS

8

> Coordination structures are unlike other phrases and are characterized by a 'coordination triangle'. Apposition structures involve the addition of constituents which are 'extra' to the sentence. Compound structures should be distinguished from superficially similar phrase structures.

In this unit we have grouped together three different kinds of construction which seem odd when compared to the structures we have looked at so far, and which require special treatment.

We begin with coordination. Coordination usually involves a closed word class, COORDINATING CONJUNCTION, which includes *and* and *or*, among others. We can see why coordination is peculiar if we consider the following sentence:

COORDINATION
Coordinating conjunction

    (1) *The man and the woman* are here.

There is normally just one noun phrase in the subject position, but here there appear to be two. In fact, there *is* just one noun phrase, because the structure is like this ('c.c.' stands for 'coordinating conjunction'):

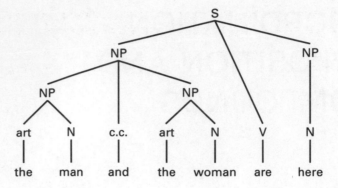

Two noun phrases have been coordinated to form a single noun phrase, which is then the single subject of the verb *are*.

Coordinate structures typically have the same structure, no matter what things are being coordinated. The structure can be symbolized like this, in the so-called 'coordination triangle':

(2)

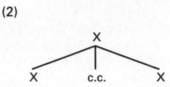

X can stand for almost any class of word or phrase, or can stand for 'sentence'. The point is that in a coordinate structure the three 'X' parts must all be of the same level (word, or phrase, or sentence) and must all be of the same class. So two nouns can be joined to make a noun (3); or two adjective phrases can be joined to make an adjective phrase (4). As (5) illustrates, three (or more) items can also be joined together.

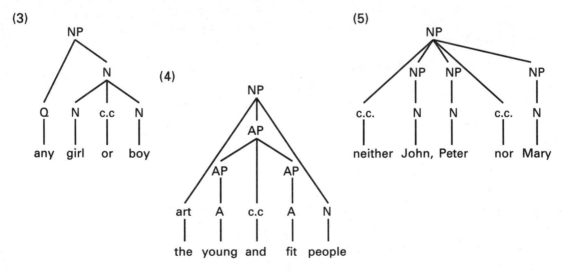

*Co*ordination can be contrasted with *sub*ordination. In coordination, two constituents are equal partners; in subordination, one constituent is inside the other:

(6) Coordination

(7) Subordination

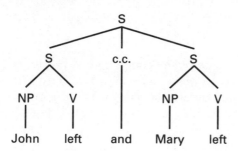

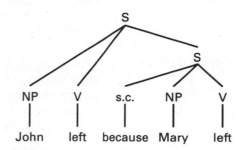

In sentence (6) two sentences are combined into a single root sentence. Neither sentence is subordinated to the other. In (7), however, the second sentence is subordinate to the first.

The following sentence illustrates another phenomenon, that of apposition:

APPOSITION

(8) I am happy, very happy.

The sentence ends in two adjective phrases, both predicative, where we would expect only one. The second phrase, *very happy*, expands on the first, as though it is an afterthought. This is an example of APPOSITION. Apposition is a bit like a coordination, where two phrases together play the part of one, but there are three major differences:

Apposition

(i) In apposition there is no special word to link parts together (i.e. nothing equivalent to a coordinating conjunction).
(ii) In apposition, the second part replaces or adds to the first, while in conjunction the two parts are added together.
(iii) In apposition, there is usually a break – a spoken pause or a comma – between the two parts.

There are various common types of apposition. One is the use of *himself*, *herself*, etc., added for emphasis after a noun phrase (not necessarily immediately after).

(9) John *himself* did this.

(10) John did this *himself*.

Or further information is given about something named by a phrase in the sentence, which might be put in brackets or surrounded by commas:

(11) The man, *the baker*, is asleep.

Apposition presents a bit of a problem when it comes to drawing a tree structure, and there is no general agreement about it among linguists. This is because a constituent added in apposition occupies a position which in a sense shouldn't exist. In (11), for example, there appear to be two noun phrases before the verb, two subjects instead of one. In exercise 3 we offer you the opportunity to explore the difference between various options for representing apposition.

COMPOUNDS

The third problematic structure is the compound. A COMPOUND is a combination of two words to make another word. Here are some examples (notice that compounds are written in different ways – sometimes with the words joined, sometimes with a hyphen, sometimes separate):

(12) a blackout

(13) a jump-cut

(14) a film-maker

(15) a table lamp

(16) an ashtray

(17) the sitting room

Compounds have a number of characteristics which distinguish them from phrases. Sometimes they involve unusual combinations of word classes, to form new word classes. For example, the adjective *black* combines with the preposition *out* to give the noun *blackout*. They can also have overall meanings which are not straightforwardly derivable from the meanings of the words they contain (unlike most phrases). This can be shown if we compare the phrase *black bird* with the compound *blackbird*:

(18) a black bird
'a bird which is black'

(19) a blackbird
'a particular kind of bird, which actually needn't be black – female blackbirds are brown'

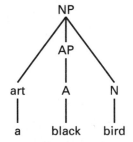
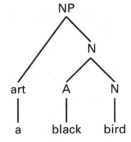

Our interest in compounds in this book is to identify them so that we can ignore them. We have drawn a tree structure for (19) to illustrate the difference from a phrase structure, but a normal sentence structure analysis would represent this instead as:

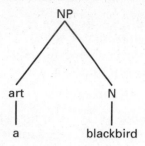

A final example to consider is:

(20) the Liverpool boat train

Here we might argue that *boat train* is a compound since the noun plus noun combination has a specific overall meaning. *Liverpool*, however, could be argued to be a separate phrase, modifying the noun *boat train*. This would give a sentence structure as follows:

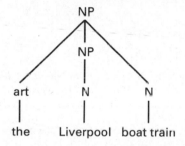

🖉 **EXERCISES**

1. Invent, using a range of different coordinating constructions:

> (a) a sentence with coordinated NPs;
> (b) a sentence with coordinated APs;
> (c) a sentence with coordinated AdvPs;
> (d) a sentence with coordinated PPs;
> (e) a sentence with coordinated Ns;
> (f) a sentence with coordinated Adjs;
> (g) a sentence with coordinated Advs;
> (h) a sentence with coordinated Ps.

2. Some closed class words can be coordinated; others cannot.

> (a) Give examples for each closed class which can be coordinated.
> (b) List the closed class words which cannot be coordinated.

> See p. 136 for a reminder of closed class words.

3. As we said earlier (pp. 85–6), there is disagreement about how to represent apposition in a tree structure. In this exercise you are asked to judge the best approach (you may find this exercise quite difficult, since it begins to treat you as an expert rather than a beginner).

(1) The man, *the baker*, is asleep.

Sentence (1) includes a noun phrase which is in apposition (italicized). Three possible tree structures for (1) are shown as Structures A, B and C. Present arguments for choosing one of these three options, and rejecting the other two.

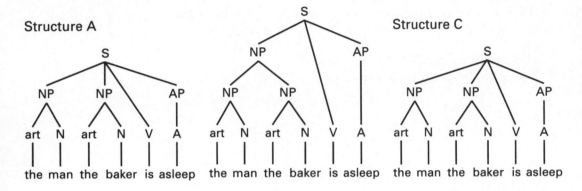

4. The word *so* is used in a range of different contexts. Examine the following sentences, and for each sentence, decide what the word class of *so* is. (It may differ from sentence to sentence.)

(1) We did it so as to leave him some food.

(2) We did it so that he would have some food.

(3) He was so in a rage that we had to leave.

(4) He did so.

(5) So he did!

(6) So what?

You may find it helpful to consult p. 136 for a list of word classes.

5. Here are some phrases (italicized) which can be used to link a sentence to a previous sentence in a discourse.

(a) Say what the class is of each phrase (it could be noun phrase, adverb phrase, adjective phrase or preposition phrase).

(b) Justify your answer by referring to the appropriate tests.

(1) They *nevertheless* decided to leave town.

(2) *In fact* it soon collapsed.

(3) *Therefore* I conclude that they entered by the back.

---

6. The sentences in this exercise illustrate different places where *not* can be put.

    (a) In each sentence *not* does something different. For each sentence try to explain what exactly *not* does; what exactly is being denied in each case?

    (b) Draw tree structures for the sentences, and try to explain why putting *not* in each place has the effect that it does.

(1) John is not saying that Mary left.

(2) John is saying that Mary did not leave.

(3) John is saying not that Mary left but that Sally left.

(4) John is saying that not Mary but Sally left.

(5) Not John but Peter is saying that Mary left.

---

7. In this data set we experiment with a subordinating structure (1) and a coordinating structure (2) to see what difference there is between them.

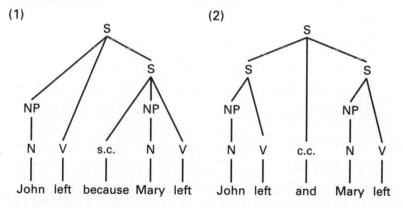

The following examples demonstrate four ways of altering the sentences.

For each type of alteration, try to explain why it has the results that it does for the two sentences – why certain alterations result in ungrammatical sentences, or why meanings change. You will find it useful to draw tree structures for each of the sentences below (trying to draw tree structures for ungrammatical sentences can help reveal why they are ungrammatical).

(a) Dropping the first verb

(1a) *John because Mary left.

(2a) John and Mary left.

(b) Dropping the second verb

(1b) *John left because Mary.

(2b) *John left and Mary.

(c) Moving the conjunction

(1c) Because John left Mary left.

(2c) *And John left Mary left.

(d) Moving the parts around the conjunction (compare the differences in meaning between (1d) and (2d) and (1) and (2).

(1d) Mary left because John left.

(2d) Mary left and John left.

---

8. Each of the following combinations can be interpreted as a phrasal combination or as a compound (like the combination of *black* + *bird*).

Draw tree structures for each version, and explain what the difference in meaning is (consult a dictionary if you aren't familiar with the compound):

(1) a green house

(2) cold cream

(3) a living room

(4) a red head

---

9. Draw tree structures for the following sentences which illustrate coordination in the languages of the corpus. For Madi and Tamil in particular you will have to decide how to draw tree structures for coordination structures unlike English.

Chinese: K1
Madi: K1, K2
Malay: K1, K2
Tamil: K1, K2

THE MANY KINDS OF NOUN PHRASE AND HOW TO ANALYSE THEM

9

Noun phrases are particularly likely to contain other phrases or sentences. These may modify the meaning of the noun phrase. It is possible to combine a range of different words or phrases at the beginning of a noun phrase. A noun phrase need not have a head; partitive phrases provide complex examples of headless noun phrases.

In a sentence, the most complex phrase is likely to be a noun phrase. For this reason, we will devote this unit to a more detailed examination of what goes on inside a noun phrase. The noun phrases we have seen so far fit into the following general pattern:

Closed class word	Phrase	The head noun	Phrase
the	old	book	
this		picture	of John
every		person	there
five	very big	crates	of apples

We begin by looking at the phrase which appears before the head, in the 'attributive' position (p. 48).

> (1) this *very exciting* news

THE MODIFYING PHRASE

While this will often be an adjective phrase, exercise 5, unit 5 (p. 55) showed that other phrases can appear here. A phrase in attributive position is said to 'modify' the head; the result of modification can be seen by comparing (1) with the phrase in (2), where *news* is not modified:

(2) this news

This very exciting news is a more specific description of the same thing that *the news* could be describing; the phrase *very exciting* in attributive position thus modifies the potential meaning of the noun phrase.

The only example of an attributive position we have seen is before the noun. But there is a second attributive position, after the noun:

(3) a man *proud of his children*

(4) the book *about John*

(3) shows an adjective phrase and (4) shows a preposition phrase; in both cases the phrases modify the noun. In exercise 8 you can explore the characteristic differences between pre- and post-noun modifiers.

(5) the book *that I read yesterday*

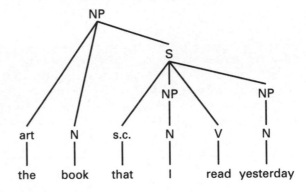

(6) some people *I met at a party*

(7) a tool *to put the painting up with*

Relative clause

A subordinate clause can be a modifier: A subordinate clause which is a modifier is called a RELATIVE CLAUSE.

Non-restrictive relative clause

A relative clause is a subordinate clause which is found in a particular place – inside a noun phrase, following the head – and makes a particular contribution to the meaning of the noun phrase which contains it. However, it is possible to have a subordinate clause which looks in almost all respects like a relative clause but which does not modify the meaning of the noun phrase:

(8) The British, *who are proud of their tomatoes*, are a nation of gourmets.

The italicized subordinate clause here looks like a relative clause, but does not modify the meaning of the noun phrase, which would have exactly the same meaning if it did not contain the clause. To see this, compare (9) and (10):

(9) the British, who are proud of their tomatoes

(10) the British

Both are noun phrases – that in (9) and that in (10) name exactly the same group of people, 'the British'. The subordinate clause adds further information about them, but does not modify the phrase. This clause is actually in apposition (see pp. 85–6); whatever solution you chose for drawing structures involving apposition should be used to draw these appositive subordinate clauses. A subordinate clause which looks like a relative clause but does not modify is called a NON-RESTRICTIVE RELATIVE CLAUSE.

Non-restrictive relative clause

We turn now to the beginning of the noun phrase. Here we may find a contained noun phrase, which ends in the suffix *-s* (or takes a form such as *my*, *his*, etc., if a pronoun), and is called a GENITIVE noun phrase. Here are some examples:

The genitive noun phrase

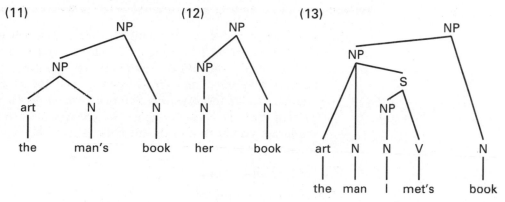

What justification can be given for these structures? Consider for example (13), put into a sentence:

(14) The man I met's book has now been published.

We can show that *the man I met's book* is a phrase, for example by substitution with *it*.

(15) It has now been published.

Inside this phrase, we can show that *the man I met's* is a phrase by substitution with *his*:

(16) His book has now been published.

A genitive noun phrase can sometimes also be moved, so that as well as saying *his book*, we can also say *that book of his*, by moving *his*.

As in the case of distinguishing root from subordinate clauses, it is important to distinguish which noun phrase contains the other. The contained noun phrase will always be the one ending in the genitive suffix *-s*, or will be a genitive form of a pronoun: *my*, *her*, *his*, *our*, *their*.

Combining different items at the beginning of a noun phrase

Here are some of the things that can be found at the beginning of a noun phrase:

(17) *the* book   *article*

(18) *that* book   *demonstrative*

(19) *every* book   *quantifier*

(20) *five* books   *numeral*

(21) *John's* book   *genitive noun phrase*

It is possible to combine some of these things, to give more complex noun phrases. The following activity asks you to explore this.

EXERCISE ✎

(a) Construct generalizations about the order in which word classes come at the beginning of a noun phrase (i.e. article, demonstrative, quantifier, numeral or genitive noun phrase). Use the noun phrases below, and invent more noun phrases to test other possibilities. Note: *do not use the word **of** in any invented example* – this changes the structure significantly and confuses the question, as we will see when we look at partitives.

(22) John's five books

(23) every two minutes

(24) his every second word

(25) the two men

(26) the many people who came

(27) all the words

(28) all John's words

(29) all those pictures

(30) those many speeches

*For example: (22) shows that the genitive noun phrase can precede the numeral. We might try inventing a noun phrase to test whether the alternative order is also possible: *five **John's** books – an ungrammatical sequence, suggesting that this order is not possible.*

(b) Say which things cannot be combined with each other at the beginning of a phrase.

*For example: can a genitive noun phrase appear in the same noun phrase as an article? – probably not, as we see from ****John's** the books* and **the **John's** books.*

Do this exercise before reading any further.

Discussion   Several things seem to be mutually exclusive. A noun phrase can contain either a genitive noun phrase or an article or a demonstrative, but in these examples these cannot be combined. But a quantifier can come either before or after any of these. And the numeral comes last – closest to the noun.

A phrase usually contains – if nothing else – its head word. But it is also possible to have a HEADLESS PHRASE – a phrase which does not contain a head. Here are some examples (noun phrase italicized):

Noun phrases without nouns
Headless phrase

(31) *The very poorest* are dying.

(32) *Some* came running.

(33) *Five* arrived quickly.

(34) *This* is my idea.

(35) *Peter's* is the best.

We know that these italicized phrases are noun phrases because they begin with things which are found only at the beginning of noun phrases – article, quantifier, numeral, demonstrative, and possessive. The structure of (31) could be drawn like this:

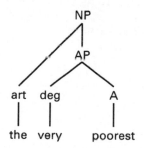

Notice that it is usually possible to fill in the missing noun, if desired, with the word *one*, giving for example *the very poorest ones*, which means more or less the same as *the very poorest*.

In the activity above where you had to work out the sequence and combination of closed class words in a noun phrase, we forbade the use of *of*. Now we explain why: once we use the word it seems that there are many more possible sequences. For example, the article can now be combined with the demonstrative:

**Partitives with
of**

(36) *a few of* those *books*

However, examples like this are misleading because they actually involve not one but *two* noun phrases. The first noun phrase is headless, and contains the second noun phrase, in a structure like this:

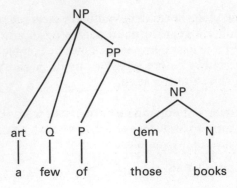

These constructions, with a headless noun phrase containing a preposition phrase with *of*, are called PARTITIVES (they usually have meanings of 'a *part* of').

EXERCISES

1. The following noun phrases contain genitive noun phrases. Draw tree structures for them which correctly put the contained noun phrase into the containing noun phrase:

(1) the man's decision

(2) an overenthusiastic official's warning

(3) his picture of John

2. Here are two noun phrases, with the same words in the same order but with different meanings, as indicated:

(1) a man's bicycle = a bicycle belonging to a particular man

(2) a man's bicycle = a type of bicycle designed for a man

(a) Draw different tree structures for (1) and for (2).
(b) Explain how your tree structures distinguish the different meanings.

3. Draw tree structures for the italicized noun phrases in the following examples. (You may find these quite difficult to analyse.)

(1) *Five of them* came back.

(2) He gave *his all*.

(3) I read it *several years ago*.

(4) *Such a thing* has never been seen before.

4. Why is the following noun phrase unusual? Draw a tree structure for this phrase as part of your explanation.

the very end

5. What class of word is *none*? In order to decide, invent several sentences with *none* in them and draw tree structures for them.

6. (a) Draw a tree structure for the italicized noun phrase in the following example.
(b) Explain what makes it unlike any noun phrase we have so far seen.

It was *so big a box* that we had to knock part of the wall down.

7. What position does the quantifier *all* occupy in this sentence?

The men *all* wanted to go.

There are several possibilities (a)–(c). Choose the correct one and justify your answer.

(a) The quantifier is directly contained in the noun phrase.

(b) The quantifier is directly contained in the sentence.

(c) The quantifier is in a noun phrase in apposition. (In the diagram below, this is indicated by not connecting it to any other part of the tree; you can choose to connect it up if you wish.)

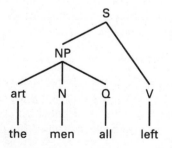

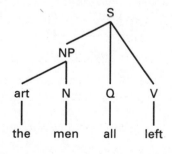

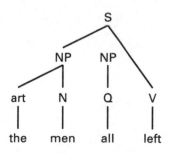

8. Some modifiers can only come *after* the noun they modify. Why? Explore this by answering the following questions, inventing examples to support your discussion:

(a) Why can a relative clause not come before the noun which it modifies?

(b) Some adjective phrases come before the noun which they modify, some come after the noun. What is the difference between them?

(c) Only a few preposition phrases can come before a noun inside a noun phrase. Which ones, and why?

---

9. Draw tree structures for the following sentences from the corpus, all of which contain noun phrases (some quite complex). If you think any of the words belong to new classes, invent class names for them.

Chinese: B1, D9
Madi: A7, D4, E1
Malay: D3, D4, D8 (Note: *yang* is not a classifier).
Tamil: D4, D7, E2

---

10.   (a) Here are some sentences containing noun phrases with relative clauses (relative clauses italicized) in English. Draw a tree structure for each whole sentence (which includes a tree structure also for the relative clause).

(1) A man *that I met* told me the museum was closed.

(2) Someone *who I talked to* said that the shops were open.

(3) The woman *I met* introduced me to her fishmonger.

(4) I just need someone *to talk to*.

(b) Now draw a tree structure for the following sentence. You will need to decide what to do about the constituent *who I talk to*. (For example, is it a relative clause?)

(5) Who I talk to is none of your business.

(c) Here are some relative clauses from other languages (relative clauses italicized). For each one, explain what the difference is between it and an equivalent English relative clause. (You may find some of these constructions difficult.)

(6) *Hebrew*

ha'is   se   pagasti   oto
the man   that   I-met   him
'the man that I met'

(7) *Bambara*

tye   ye   ne   ye   no   min   ye   san
man   *past*   I   *past*   horse   which   see   buy
'The man bought the horse that I saw.'

(**ye** *indicates past tense; there is another word* **ye** *which means 'see'.*)

(8) *Hindi*

admi-ne   jis   caku-se   murgi-ko   mara tha,
man   which   knife-with   chicken   killed

us   caku-ko   Ram-ne   dekha
that   knife   Ram   saw

'Ram saw the knife that the man killed the chicken with.'

10 REORDERING THE PARTS OF A SENTENCE

> A phrase or word can be moved to the beginning of a sentence, with different effects depending on what is moved. A passive sentence can be derived from an active sentence by moving part of it. Case-marking is a potential way of indicating which noun phrase is subject and which is object.

On p. 4 we introduced a 'movement test' for phrase structure. If a group of words can be moved together, they are likely to constitute a phrase (or subordinate clause). In this unit we look at the kinds of 'movement' which can happen to the constituents of a sentence.

TOPICAL- IZATION

Movement of a phrase to the beginning of the sentence
A simple example of movement can be seen in (2), compared to (1).

(1) I like John.

(2) John, I like.

In (2), the object of the verb has been put at the front of the sentence, in this case for emphasis. Moving a phrase to the beginning of the sentence (to the left of the subject) is called TOPICALIZATION when it is for the purpose of emphasis.

YES-NO QUESTIONS

Movement of a verb to the beginning of the sentence
Another example of movement to the beginning of the sentence can be seen by comparing (3) with (4):

(3) Mary was happy.

(4) Was Mary happy?

(4) is a YES-NO QUESTION, so called because it can be answered with 'Yes' or 'No'. It involves movement of the verb to the beginning of the sentence. In modern English only a few verbs can be moved in this way – the modal verbs, the auxiliary verbs, and the main verbs *be* and (in some dialects) *have*. In the case of other main verbs, the auxiliary *do* is added and moved instead to the beginning of the sentence.

(5) Peter saw Mary yesterday.

(6) *Did* Peter see Mary yesterday?

It is also possible to create a yes-no question without moving anything. By saying (5) with a particular intonation (e.g. raising your voice), it is possible to make it into a question.

Movement of a *wh*-phrase to the beginning of the sentence

INFORMATION QUESTIONS

Another kind of question involves the movement of a phrase to the beginning of a sentence:

(7) *What* did you see?

(8) *Which book* did you read?

(9) *Which* did you read?

(10) *Where* did you put it?

(11) *In whose house* did you stay?

These sentences are all examples of an INFORMATION QUESTION. In an information question a phrase is moved to the beginning of a sentence in order to request a particular kind of information (the specific kind of information relates to the class of the moved phrase). Here is a sample tree structure:

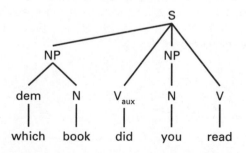

Why do we say that the phrase has been 'moved'? This has been a source of much theoretical discussion, which it is not appropriate to explain in detail here. However, a simple reason can be given. *Which book* is a substitute for the object of the verb *read*. Normally we would expect the object to follow the verb. Because *which book* is at the beginning of the sentence instead of after the verb we say that it has moved (it is a similar process to topicalization). This argument works best with cases where the object is moved (e.g. (7)–(9)), and is slightly weaker in the case of preposition phrases (e.g. (10) and (11)) which are less rigidly positioned (though we would still normally expect a preposition phrase to follow the verb).

Wh-word

The phrase which is moved in an information question has a special kind of component: it contains a WH-WORD. *Wh*-words are not a word class of their own, but a sub-type of various different word classes (they are called *wh*-words because they have a distinctive shape, as most of them begin with *wh*-):

Some English wh-*words*	*Word class*
who	noun (like a pronoun)
whose	noun (like a genitive pronoun)
where	noun (like the nouns *here* or *there*)
what	demonstrative
which	demonstrative

Wh-words can be alone as the head of a phrase as in (7), or can accompany a head as in (8), or can be a closed class word in a headless phrase as in (9).

Passive sentences as examples of movement

(12)–(14) illustrate the difference between PASSIVE and ACTIVE sentences.

(12) *The meat pie* was eaten yesterday.   (passive)

(13) *The meat pie* was eaten *by John* yesterday.

(passive)

(14) *John* ate *the meat pie* yesterday.   (active)

The difference between active and passive sentences can be understood by thinking of a passive sentence as the result in part of movement. (This is not obviously the right account, but it has frequently been proposed, and does help clarify the construction.) Here is how it works. Take (14), and move the object to the subject position; take the original subject and either drop it completely (Option A) or put it in a preposition phrase (Option B):

Option A

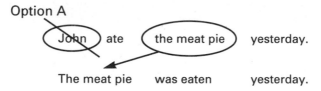

Option B

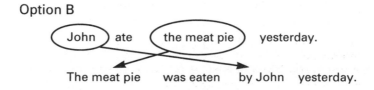

So the crucial characteristic of a passive sentence is that the 'normal' (i.e. in an active sentence) object is now in subject position. Passive sentences also have a characteristic morphology of the verb, and often make use of auxiliary verbs, like *was* in the above example.

It is important for the person who hears or reads a sentence to be able to work out which noun phrase is the subject and which is the object. For example, in sentence (15), we can only understand who the eater is and what is the thing eaten once we identify *the lion* as the subject and *the tiger* as the object:

Case and the role of a noun phrase

> (15) The lion ate the tiger.

In an English sentence like (15) we know which noun phrase is the subject and which is the object because of *where they are in the sentence.*

But sometimes it is the form of the words which tells us which is subject and object. In (16) we know that *I* is the subject not only by position but also because *I* is a pronoun which is found only in subject position.

> (16) I met him.

This means that even if we jumbled the words into a sentence which is unacceptable we still know which is the subject and which the object, and can understand the sentence even if we do not accept it:

> (17) *him met I.

In English, we rely almost exclusively on the position of words and phrases as a way of expressing and working out the meaning of a sentence – for example, as a way of distinguishing the subject and the object. The pronoun *I* is untypical. But in some languages, other words change as well. For example, in German, an article can change depending on whether it is in a subject noun phrase or an object noun phrase; in a 'masculine' noun phrase, the article corresponding to 'the' is *der* or *den* depending on whether the noun phrase is subject or object:

> (18)

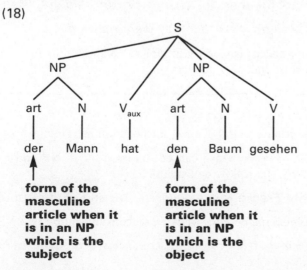

Case-marking

This alteration in the morphology of the word as a way of expressing whether a phrase is subject or object is an example of CASE-MARKING. For example, *der* is said to be marked with the 'nominative' case, thereby indicating that it is the subject. And *den* is said to be marked with the 'accusative' case, thereby indicating that it is the object. Where the subject and the object are indicated by case-marking, there is less need to indicate them by always putting them in the same positions (as in English). For example, in German it would also be possible to say:

(19) *Den*   Baum   hat   *der*   Mann   gesehen

     the   tree   has   the   man   seen

     'the man has seen the tree.'

Though the noun phrases have changed position, we still know that *der Mann* is the subject because the article in the phrase has nominative case.

EXERCISES ✎

We are almost at the end of the book; you should be increasingly able to take on new sentence structure phenomena by yourself, and it is increasingly appropriate for you to build your own arguments. For this reason, several of the exercises which follow introduce new phenomena from English.

1. The examples discussed so far have all involved movement to the beginning of the sentence. But it can be argued that in some sentences a phrase or subordinate clause is moved to the end of a sentence. Here are three such examples:

(1) I gave to Peter *the big box of books which was in the attic.*

(2) I met the man yesterday *who you said you liked.*

(3) It was obvious *that they were married.*

For each sentence, provide an argument to show that the italicized phrase or clause has been moved.

2.

    teach, donate, sell, buy, tell, throw, demonstrate

This is a list of verbs which can be followed by an NP and a PP in sequence, as in the following example:

I taught *French to the children.* (NP and PP italicized)

(a) Which of these verbs can also be followed by two NPs?

*For example: **teach** can, as we see in **I taught the children French**.*

(b) The verbs which do *not* have an NP–NP order have something in common which differentiates them from the others. What is it? (Clue: look at the form of the words.)

---

3. Like an information question, a relative clause can begin with a phrase containing a *wh*-word, which might be argued to have moved. The following noun phrases all contain a relative clause, which has been italicized to help you:

(1) the books *I lent to you*

(2) the books *that I lent to you*

(3) the books *which I lent to you*

(4) the boy *who I saw*

(5) the singer *whose voice I like the best*

(6) the person *in whose house I stayed*

(7) the place *where I met you*

(8) the time *when I ate five lobsters*

(a) Circle the word or phrase which comes before the subject inside each relative clause. (For example, circle *that* in (2).)

(b) The subordinate clauses in (3)–(8) have a phrase at the beginning which includes a *wh*-word. Compare each relative clause with an information question which resembles it; what general differences are there between a relative clause and an information question?

*For example, you would compare the relative clause **which I lent to you** with the information question **Which did I lend to you?***

(c) What class of word is *that* in (2)? Justify your answer, and draw a tree structure for (2).

---

4. In the following examples, sentence (a) is active, and sentence (b) is passive. Sentence (c) shows a third possibility; here the object of the equivalent active sentence is in the subject position (like passive) but there is no auxiliary verb or special passive morphology.

(1)   a. I melted the ice.

      b. The ice was melted (by me).

      c. The ice melted.

(2)   a. The submarine sank the ship.

      b. The ship was sunk.

      c. The ship sank.

(3) a. Maxine received the parcel.

b. The parcel was received.

c. *The parcel received.

(4) a. The men resembled aliens.

b. *Aliens were resembled.

c. *Aliens resembled.

(a) Some verbs can appear in all three kinds of sentence, some can appear only in types (a) and (b), while some can appear only in type (a). Try to explain why.

(b) Explain why *The lion killed* cannot mean that the lion ended up dead. (Compare *The ship sank* (2c) where the ship ends up sunk.)

---

5. It is possible to make a passive sentence by combining *be* with the passive participle. It is also possible to use *get* (or in the past tense *got*) instead:

(1) This carpet gets cleaned once a month.

(2) The food got eaten by John.

What is the word class of *get*? Justify your answer.

---

6. In each of the following sentences, *how* or a phrase beginning with *how* acts to subordinate a sentence. The subordinate clauses are italicized to help you.

(1) I asked her *how quickly he was running*.

(2) I asked her *how hot it was*.

(3) I asked her *how he seemed*.

(a) Draw tree structures for these sentences. This involves deciding whether *how* is part of a whole phrase at the front of the sentence, or whether it is on its own.

(b) What is the word class of *how* in each sentence? (It may be different in different sentences.)

(c) Is there any justification for saying that the phrase containing *how* has been moved to the beginning of the subordinate clause?

---

7. In different languages, information questions are dealt with differently. For example, the question phrase (*wh*-phrase) may not move, or might move to a position other than the front of the sentence.

Examine the languages in the corpus and for each language determine how information questions are formed.

You should look particularly at:

Chinese : B1-3
Madi: B1-7
Malay: B1-5
Tamil: B1-10

---

8. Not all languages form passive in the same way that English does. Examine the languages in the corpus and for each language.

(a) Determine whether there is a difference in sentence structure (or morphology) between the equivalent of English active/passive sentences.
(b) If there is a difference, describe it.

You should look particularly at:

Chinese: L1, L2
Madi: L1-4
Malay A2, A3, L1-3
Tamil A4, L1

---

9. Tamil has fairly free phrase order. Examine the Tamil sentences in the corpus and describe:

(a) Where the verb typically goes.
(b) Where the subject and object noun phrases go.
(c) How the placement of phrases relates to what is being emphasized?
(d) Why Tamil is able to have freer word order than English?

11 IS THERE A VERB PHRASE?

It might be argued that there is a verb phrase, containing the verb and its object, plus other things which follow the verb. Evidence for or against this idea is presented in the form of exercises.

We have seen four kinds of phrase in English sentence structures: noun phrase, adjective phrase, adverb phrase and preposition phrase. Many linguists would argue for a fifth kind of phrase: a verb phrase. The verb phrase includes the verb, its object, and various other things which follow it. The verb, on this account, is the head of the verb phrase and not the head of the sentence. Here is a tree structure which illustrates what a verb phrase would look like:

(1)

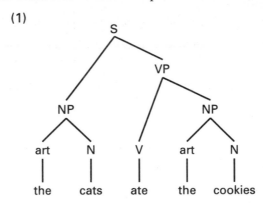

The division of a sentence into a noun phrase and a verb phrase, like this, fits with a traditional approach to sentence structure, which divides the sentence into the subject (the noun phrase) and the predicate (the verb and object, etc.; i.e. the verb phrase). The claims of traditional grammar are not always right, and there has been much discussion in recent work on sentence structure about whether there is a verb phrase, in English or in other languages. In this unit you will become engaged in this debate, by working through various suggestive examples, to decide whether they provide evidence for or against a verb phrase. You may find after working through all of these exercises that there is some evidence for and some against; if you do find this, make a decision based on the weight of evidence for or against. This unit illustrates one of the basic claims of this book – that the study of sentence structure is a problem-solving activity.

 **EXERCISES**

1. (1) He is hungry for meat.

(2) He hungers for meat.

(a) Show that *hungry for meat* is an adjective phrase.
(b) How might this provide evidence for a verb phrase in (2)? (Clue: recall the discussion of cross-phrase generalizations, p. 61.)

2. With the exception of imperatives a root sentence always contains a subject, but need not contain an object. Hence while (2) with a missing object is grammatical, (3) with a missing subject is ungrammatical.

	subject		*object*
(1)	The man	was eating	cheese.
(2)	The man	was sleeping.	
(3)		*Was eating	cheese.

Explain why this provides evidence that there is a verb phrase. (Clue: consider the characteristic sorts of structure which any phrase can have.)

3. The italicized constituent in the following acceptable sentence is somewhat problematic.

His finally eating the food is a relief to all of us.

The initial genitive noun phrase *his* suggests that the italicized constituent is a noun phrase. Assume that this is true.

(a) Draw a tree structure for this constituent, without a verb phrase.
(b) Draw a tree structure for this constituent, using a verb phrase.
(c) Explain why the tree structure using the verb phrase fits better with the typical structures of phrases which we have so far seen.

4.   (1) I never wanted to read it, but read it I did.

(2) I never wanted to read it, but I did.

(3) I asked him to eat the potato, so eat the potato he did.

Why do sentences (1)–(3) suggest the existence of a verb phrase? (Clue: consider the tests for phrase structure.)

---

5. If (there is no verb phrase and) the verb is the head of the sentence, it is unlike other heads. Explain why. (There are several differences.)

---

6. The auxiliary verbs and modal verbs are closed sub-classes of the open word class 'verb'. We have not so far claimed that these types of verb are a head.

The pronouns are similarly a closed sub-class of the open word class 'noun'. But pronouns *do* head noun phrases.

Assume that an auxiliary verb *can* be a head. Why does this provide evidence in favour of a verb phrase?

---

7. A sentence can resemble a noun phrase. Here are some examples:

(1) The wolves observed the travellers silently.

(2) the wolves' silent observation of the travellers

(3) The president gave the medal to the children.

(4) the president's gift of the medal to the children

(a) Explain why, if there is a verb phrase, the parallel between a sentence and a noun phrase (discussed on p. 61) is weakened somewhat.

(b) Suggest a way of rethinking the structure of a noun phrase, so that the parallel between sentence and noun phrase is restored. Present any evidence for your rethinking.

---

8. In unit 5, exercise 5 we saw that various phrases can be put before a noun inside a noun phrase.

(a) Work out the word class of *running* in the following noun phrase, and draw a tree structure for the noun phrase.

(1) The running man

(b) Why does this example support the idea that there is a verb phrase?

(c) The following noun phrase is ungrammatical. Does this argue *against* a verb phrase? (Consider in this light your answer to unit 5, exercise 5b.)

(2) *the running away man

Now that you have completed these exercises you should be able to come to a decision for yourself about whether there is a verb phrase in the English sentence. (You may then need to decide whether there is a verb phrase in other languages.) Though there is likely to be more evidence which you have not yet considered, for practical reasons you have to make a decision on this question of syntactic structure. Up to now in this book we have not used a verb phrase, because it made it simpler to teach the structure of sentences. This may not have been the ultimately correct approach. Only you can decide. This illustrates one of the basic points of this book – that grammar is a problem-solving discipline.

Is there a verb phrase?

12 LINGUISTIC THEORY AND SENTENCE STRUCTURE

> The account of sentence structure outlined in this book has been based on the findings of generative grammars. Generative grammars are associated with questions about what it means to know a language.

This book has outlined a way of thinking about sentence structure. It is based on the idea that a sentence is divided into constituents which do not overlap, every constituent belonging to a class. Tests of replacement and movement, among others, have been suggested as a way of discovering constituent structure and the class of a constituent. We have proposed that meaning is not a reliable guide either to constituent structure or to classification. These are all hypotheses, and some of them might be wrong. Perhaps we could argue, for example, that some phrases do not belong to any class; or that there is a much larger number of word classes; or perhaps phrases *do* overlap. It is because these are hypotheses rather than unquestionable laws that this book has shown you how to solve sentence structure problems by yourself, so that you can better judge which among competing hypotheses is the best.

The approach to sentence structure in this book has not been overtly theoretical. However, it has been based on some of the findings of linguistic theories, particularly the theories known as 'generative grammars'. In this final unit, we explore some of the ideas about sentence structure which have been produced within generative grammars. This unit is completely different in its aims from the rest of the book; for a moment, we speculate rather than attempt to solve specific sentence structure problems.

A generative grammar for the English language can be thought of as a collection of generalizations which can be used to decide whether a particular sentence is grammatical in English. We can illustrate this statement with an extremely simple example involving a made-up language called 'L'. The grammar consists of just one generalization (also called a RULE).

What a generative grammar is

Rule

These are all the possible sentences in a language which we'll call L (i.e. the language consists of just four sentences):

> Y
>
> X Y
>
> Y Z
>
> X Y Z

The generative grammar could look like this:

> Every sentence in the language L fits into the following pattern:
>
> > (X) Y (Z)
>
> (*A letter in brackets is optional*).

This grammar will tell us that X Y Z is a grammatical sentence and Y is a grammatical sentence, but it will tell us that neither Z Y nor X Z is a grammatical sentence.

A generative grammar of English is conceptually similar, but of course a lot more complicated, because there are many more sentences, and they are much more complex. The grammar should be able to state for any sentence whether it is a grammatical sentence of the language.

Generative grammars might differ from each other in any aspect, including both the kinds of rule used and the details of individual rules. Fairly current generative grammars which are significantly different from each other include Government-Binding Theory, Generalized Phrase Structure Grammar, Relational Grammar and Lexical-Functional Grammar. Some older generative grammars (which still have some proponents, but have mainly been superseded) include Generative Semantics, and the Extended Standard Theory. Because the rules in a generative grammar are a very detailed set of predictions about a language, the grammar is therefore subject to constant modification when any of its predictions are found to be wrong; grammars have tended to last about ten years before they require a fundamental rethinking. In principle, each new generative grammar is a better theory than the one which it replaces; there will usually be several competing grammars at any one time.

The *Syntactic Structures* generative grammar for English

Phrase structure rule

What does a generative grammar for English actually look like? We will illustrate this by giving some snapshots of the earliest generative grammar, proposed by Noam Chomsky in his first book *Syntactic Structures* (1957). The grammar generates sentences (i.e. judges their grammaticality) by means of two kinds of rule. The first kind is a PHRASE STRUCTURE RULE. Here are some examples (note that they assume a verb phrase ('VP')):

S	$\longrightarrow$	NP VP
NP	$\longrightarrow$	art N
VP	$\longrightarrow$	V NP
art	$\longrightarrow$	the, a
N	$\longrightarrow$	man, horse
V	$\longrightarrow$	saw

These are 'rewriting rules'. The idea is that every sentence starts out as an S. An S can then be rewritten as an NP followed by a VP. An NP can be rewritten as an article followed by a noun. A noun can be rewritten as *man*, and so on. By this means, S is eventually rewritten as one of a number of different possible English sentences. A tree structure diagram of the kind used in this book illustrates how the S has been rewritten into its components (the tree structure diagram records the stages of rewriting).

Transformational rule

The second kind of rule is a TRANSFORMATIONAL RULE. A transformational rule can change a tree structure into a different one. For example, it can change the tree structure for the sentence *a man saw the horse* into the tree structure for the sentence *the horse was seen by a man*. The rule might look like this:

Take a sequence $NP_1 + V_{past} + NP_2$ and change it into a sequence $NP_2 + was + V_{passive} + by + NP_1$.

That is, it changes any active sentence into an equivalent passive sentence (see pp. 102–3). It was the use of transformational rules that made *Syntactic Structures* such a revolutionary theory of sentence structure. Transformational rules were introduced into the grammar for various reasons. One reason is that a transformational rule is a way of expressing the fact that an active and a passive form of a sentence mean more or less the same, despite having different structures. It is because of the idea of transformational rules that we talked in this book about 'moving' parts of a sentence. A type of generative grammar which has transformational rules is called a

Transformational generative grammar

TRANSFORMATIONAL GENERATIVE GRAMMAR.

Modifying the *Syntactic Structures* grammar

All generative grammars can be seen as developments of the *Syntactic Structures* grammar. Here is just one example. Transformational rules tend to overgenerate – that is, they make incorrect predictions. For example, the rule we outlined above would take (1) and change it into (2):

(1) I saw myself.

(2) *Myself was seen by me.

Since (2) is not acceptable to a speaker of English, the grammar should not predict that it is grammatical. So we need to add a rule which says that (2) and sentences like it are ungrammatical. Here is such a rule:

> If a reflexive pronoun (like *myself*) and a noun phrase (like *I*) refer to the same person, the reflexive pronoun must follow the noun phrase.

This is neither a phrase structure rule nor a transformational rule. It could be seen instead as a rule which 'constrains' (limits the activity of) another rule. Much of the work in generative grammar over the past 30 years has been devoted increasingly to constraints along these sorts of lines.

There is a problem which confronts any generative grammar of a human language. This is that while the grammar can always state whether a particular sentence is grammatical or not, it is sometimes less straightforward for a speaker of the language to decide whether the sentence is acceptable. For example, the grammaticality/acceptability of the following sentences (and similar) has been used to test predictions made by certain generative grammars. Read them and decide which *you* think are acceptable.

IDEALIZATION

(3) Which books did you put on the shelves before reading?

(4) Which books did you put them on the shelves before reading?

(5) Which books did you put on the shelves before reading them?

The characteristic pattern of sentence (3) is that the 'moved' phrase *which books* appears to be the object of two verbs (*put* and *reading*), rather than the normal single verb. (4) and (5) alter the sentence by filling in each of the two object positions, so that the 'moved' phrase now is the object of only one verb. Before the late 1970s, it seems that no one had ever asked whether sentences with these particular patterns were grammatical or not. If you collected examples of sentences which are actually produced by speakers or writers, you might not find any examples of these at all. So they are quite marginal in terms of actual linguistic behaviour; furthermore, some people find that they are not immediately sure about the acceptability of the sentences. Nevertheless, despite these two differences between the sentences 'for the grammar' and the sentences 'for the speaker', they were for a while extremely important for certain developments in generative grammar. Going back to the sentences, the predictions were that (3) is grammatical, (4) is ungrammatical, and (5) is grammatical: many, though not all, speakers agree that (5) is acceptable, (4) is unacceptable, and (3) is somewhere in between. The crucial question is whether the 'in between' (3) falls into the grammatical or the ungrammatical class: a generative grammar must decide between these two poles without being able to make a middle prediction. (There have been certain kinds of generative grammar which have explored the possibility of predicting 'in-between' grammaticality; however, this shift has been argued by some to be a shift away from the central tenets of generative grammars into a new kind of non-generative grammar.)

This is an extreme example, but it illustrates the basic point quite well. Linguists tend to assume that the grammar they build will judge the grammaticality of an idealization: an abstract form of the language, which will differ in certain details from any actual manifestations of the language (the hope is that the differences are basically irrelevant to the concerns of the grammar). The question of idealization occurs whenever there is an attempt to build an abstract theory of any aspect of human behaviour: inevitably there is not a perfect match.

A difference between people in whether they use or accept a particular sentence

Sometimes a question of acceptability can be a source of disagreement between different speakers of a language. This can relate to dialect or standardization.

DIALECT

Many languages are subdivided into dialects, each dialect usually associated with a different geographical region where the language is spoken. (Sometimes, as in the case of Chinese, there is disagreement about whether, for example, Cantonese and Hokkai are different dialects or actually different languages.) Usually, there will be fairly small differences between dialects in the generalizations about sentence structures. Two people who apparently speak the same language might disagree with each other about acceptability because they speak different dialects. Here are two examples of sentences acceptable in some dialects but not others. (In my dialect, neither sentence is acceptable, in the sense that I would not say either of them.)

(6) Have you any money?

(7) To whom did you give the money?

In (6), the main verb *have* is moved in a yes-no question (I would use *do* instead), while in (7) the *wh*-word *whom* is used after a preposition (I would use *who*). Another example of difference between dialects can be seen in the use of *didnae* in some Scottish and northern English dialects; this appears at first sight to be identical in its sentence structure function to *didn't*. But *didnae* is not covered by exactly the same generalizations; so that while (8) is acceptable, (9) is not. (If you substitute *didn't* you should find that both sentences are acceptable.)

(8) She didnae go.

(9) *Didnae she go?

Thus for different dialects of English, there are different generalizations in some cases (usually involving things like auxiliary verbs), and this can lead to disagreement *across* dialects about acceptability.

In many languages, some dialects become more prominent than others. Difference of prominence between dialects is always for historical reasons. (For example, the dialect is prominent because it is spoken by the people in power.) The prominence is impossible to justify on the basis of internal differences (e.g. in sentence structure) between the dialects. A prominent dialect is sometimes named as a STANDARD of the language (e.g. Standard English), and it is common for rules to be invented which regulate this standard in certain ways. These might include rules about sentence structure, rules about choice of words or particular morphologies, or rules about pronunciation (focusing specifically on accent). Grammars which consist of such regulations are called PRESCRIPTIVE GRAMMARS, and are differentiated from the kind of grammar explored in this book which is a DESCRIPTIVE GRAMMAR. The regulations in prescriptive grammars might, for example, include:

STANDARD-IZATION

Prescriptive grammar

Descriptive grammar

> Do not begin a sentence with *and*.
> Do not end a sentence with a preposition.
> Do not use a 'double negative' (e.g. *I can't get no satisfaction*).

I have ignored regulations of this kind in this book; in fact, like every other English user, I have probably broken them at times. I have ignored them partly because they are irrelevant to our aims, which are to describe English as people actually use it. In addition, some of them fail on their own terms; notoriously, the rule 'Do not end a sentence with a preposition', invented in the seventeenth century, results in some clearly unacceptable sentences, as in (10), compared with the acceptable (11) which breaks the rule:

(10) This is something up with which I will not put.

(11) This is something which I will not put up with.

The rules of prescriptive grammar are 'cultural debris', the result of decisions made in the past which have been repeated up to the present. Their function is to symbolize a particular way of using English as 'standard'. You are unlikely to find any basis in the present book for justifying any of these rules.

Generative grammar and knowledge of language

We said above that:

> A generative grammar for the English language can be thought of as a collection of generalizations which can be used to decide whether a particular sentence is grammatical in English.

A generative grammar's generalizations are written on paper, and referred to by a linguist. However, since the early 1960s, shortly after generative grammars were first proposed, people have wondered whether a speaker of a language also somehow refers to a set of generalizations in her or his mind. This set of generalizations would resemble a generative grammar, and would be a kind of (unconsciously activated) knowledge. What would the generalizations – the 'mental generative grammar' – actually do for a speaker? It would for example enable the speaker to speak and write sentences which automatically (i.e. without conscious deliberation) fit into the patterns of the language; and it would enable the speaker to decide whether particular sentences were acceptable.

It is this line of thinking which makes the study of sentence structure of fundamental interest for the study of what human minds are like. The line has been taken further still: if a person has a mental generative grammar, perhaps some aspects of that generative grammar are innate, that is they are genetically inherited as part of being human. This would make our knowledge of language like our knowledge of vision. (We probably inherit some aspects of our ability to understand what we see.) Speculations along these lines take us from the study of sentence structure into fundamental philosophical questions; these questions are particularly associated with the inventor of generative grammars, Noam Chomsky.

There are two distinct issues as regards this line of enquiry into knowledge of language. The first relates to what a person's knowledge of language is when they know English (for example). The second relates to what a person's knowledge of language is as a result of genetic inheritance. The two kinds of knowledge are clearly different: there is nothing genetically inherited about most aspects of English. But there may be certain fundamental principles of the knowledge of English which are inherited – such as perhaps the principle that English sentences involve non-intersecting phrases. Maybe *every* human language involves non-intersecting phrases; this might then be a genetically inherited element of our knowledge of language. Being able to inherit certain fundamentals of knowledge of language would give all human children a head start in learning their first language – no matter what language is being learned, whether English, Sanskrit, Navajo, or Mayan.

Final comments

This unit has shifted from the working out of generalizations about English sentences of units 1–11 to looking at profound questions about what a person knows when she or he knows a language. But despite the sharp change of focus, the concerns of this unit grow out of the practices discussed in the rest of the book.

You should now be ready to move from the relatively informal study of sentence structure into a study of the theories which have been developed in linguistics to study sentence structure – the theories of SYNTAX.

FURTHER READING

INTRODUCTORY

Brown, E.K. and Miller, J.E., *Syntax: A Linguistic Introduction to Sentence Structure* (HarperCollins, London, 1980).
An overview, referring explicitly to linguistic theory, of issues introduced in the present book (but in much greater detail).

Chomsky, Noam, *Language and Problems of Knowledge: The Managua Lectures* (MIT Press, Cambridge, MA, 1988).
The wider implications of the study of sentence structure. Includes a discussion of why it is important to ask whether or not there is a verb phrase.

Newmeyer, Frederick, *Linguistic Theory in America* (2nd edn, Academic Press, New York, 1986).
A history of generative grammars, including a straightforward introduction to the conceptual issues which underlie these kinds of theory of sentence structure, and clear accounts of the kinds of rule and generalization which have been proposed.

Sells, Peter, *Lectures on Contemporary Syntactic Theory* (CSLI Publications, Stanford, CA, 1985).
Subtitled 'An Introduction to Government-Binding Theory, Generalized Phrase Structure Grammar, and Lexical-Functional Grammar', this book gives clear summaries of some major generative grammars which emerged in the 1980s. A good brief overview of what relatively complete theories of sentence structure look like.

INTERMEDIATE

Chomsky, Noam, *Syntactic Structures* (Mouton, The Hague, 1957).
A classic, the book which invented a whole new way of doing linguistics. Most of the specific theory proposed is now obsolete, but the general discussion of how a theory of sentence structure can be constructed remains indispensable.

Comrie, Bernard, *Language Universals and Linguistic Typology: Syntax and Morphology* (Blackwell, Oxford, 1981).
A discussion of the similarities between languages, and how they should be dealt with by a linguistic theory. Chapters on word order, subject, case-marking, relative clauses, etc.

Haegeman, Liliane, *Introduction to Government and Binding Theory* (Blackwell, Oxford, 1991).
Government-Binding Theory has probably become the most influential theory of sentence structure. There are a number of good introductions to it, and this is one of them.

Halliday, M. A. K., *An Introduction to Functional Grammar* (Arnold, London, 1985).
This is an introduction (by its originator) to an alternative non-generative way of thinking about sentence structure, an approach which has been very influential – particularly among those who are interested in text analysis (including the application of linguistics to literature).

Shopen, Timothy, (ed.) *Language Typology and Syntactic Description* (3 vols, Cambridge University Press, Cambridge, 1985).
An investigation of kinds of sentence structure in the world's languages, organized according to topic. Chapters on word classes, subordinate clauses, subjects and objects, etc.

Spencer, Andrew, *Morphological Theory* (Blackwell, Oxford, 1991).
Though concerned with the forms of words, Spencer points to the many situations where the form of a word has a relevance for sentence structure. Includes a chapter on compounds.

ADVANCED

Baltin, Mark R. and Kroch, Anthony S. (eds), *Alternative Conceptions of Phrase Structure* (Chicago University Press, Chicago, 1989).
Huck, Geoffrey J. and Almerido, E. Ojeda (eds), *Syntax and Semantics 20: Discontinuous Constituency* (Academic Press, New York, 1987).
Two collections of essays of considerable theoretical complexity, presenting ideas about sentence structure from the perspective of different generative grammars, and using examples from a wide variety of languages.

Jackendoff, Ray, *X̄ Syntax: A Study of Phrase Structure* (MIT Press, Cambridge, MA, 1977).
X-bar theory is a theory of phrase structures; its basic idea is that phrases have complex internal structure (much more complex than outlined in the present book), and that phrases of different classes resemble each other in interesting ways. This book outlines a particular version of X-bar theory and presents detailed analyses of English sentences.

Speas, Margaret, *Phrase Structure in Natural Language* (Kluwer, Dordrecht, 1990).
An overview of contemporary views about sentence structure, including theoretical discussion of rules for building structure. There is a particular focus on languages which, unlike English, have relatively unrestricted word and phrase order.

REFERENCE BOOKS

Crystal, David, *The Cambridge Encyclopedia of Language* (Cambridge University Press, Cambridge, 1987).
An illustrated survey of language and linguistics for the general reader, and a useful compendium of information for anyone working on language or linguistics. Introductory.

Asher, R. *et al.* (eds), *The Encyclopedia of Language and Linguistics* (10 vols, Pergamon and Aberdeen University Press, 1993).
Bright, William (ed.), *International Encyclopedia of Linguistics* (4 vols, Oxford University Press, Oxford, 1992).
Two reference works, with articles on many of the topics covered in the present book, from the perspective of linguistic theory. Introductory to intermediate.

Quirk, Randolph and Greenbaum, Sidney, *A University Grammar of English* (Longman, London, 1973).
Quirk, R., Greenbaum, S., Leech, G. and Svartvik, J., *A Comprehensive Grammar of the English Language* (Longman, London, 1985).
Respectively shorter and longer versions of one of the major contemporary descriptive grammars of English. Not for the most part based on the findings of generative linguistics, and presenting different analyses in some cases from the analyses argued for in the present book.

PROJECTS

You should be able to do these projects after completing the book. They involve you in analysing actual sentences. You will find that some are more complicated than the ones analysed in this book, and you will find some problems which we have not addressed (such as words whose word classes you are not sure about); however, you should by now have the basic problem-solving skills to be able to confront and deal with these problems.

1 Different kinds of text typically use different kinds of language, which include different vocabularies and different sentence structures; these differences are called differences in REGISTER. You can use your knowledge of sentence structure to explore some of these differences. Here is one way of doing it: pick a poem written in the nineteenth century, a newspaper article written today, and an academic book (e.g. a textbook). Write out the first sentence (not the title) from each text, and draw a tree structure for it. Now do the same with another three texts of the same kind. Do you see any patterns of difference emerging?

2 Choose an English sentence discussed in this book, and get it translated into another language. Can the sentence be translated word-for-word (in the same order)? There are likely to be some differences; try to work out what those differences tell you about more general differences between English and the other language. This exercise can be repeated many times; it will give you one way of beginning to understand the structure of the second language.

3 Look at a guide to English usage or a prescriptive grammar (as discussed in unit 12), and examine in particular the sentences which you are advised not to use. Try to explain why the guide advises you not to use a particular type of sentence. Draw

a tree structure for an example of the forbidden sentence type, and compare it with a tree structure of an acceptable version of the sentence. Is it possible to show that one sentence is better than the other on the basis of the structural difference between them? (For example, can you show that one structure is more effective at communicating its meaning than the other?) This exercise can be repeated many times. Note that some people think that there are no value differences of this kind between sentences; this exercise should give you a basis for coming to a decision by yourself.

4 Different dialects of English can differ in a number of ways, most obviously in accent – the pronunciation of the language – and in vocabulary. There may also be some differences in sentence structure between two dialects of English. Try to find equivalent sentences from two dialects which are structurally different (e.g. the words or phrases are in a different order). Draw a tree structure for each sentence, and describe the difference in syntactic terms (e.g. discuss word class, generalizations about order, processes such as movement which might be involved, and so on). (An example of such a difference, involving the possibility of having sentence-initial *didnae* compared to *didn't* is discussed on pp. 116–17.)

SENTENCES FROM OTHER LANGUAGES

A CORPUS is a representative collection of things, and the four corpuses (or 'corpora') which follow present collections of relatively simple sentences from four different kinds of language. For each language, sentences are given with rough English translations of what the sentence as a whole means. In order to work with the sentences, you need to decide what the individual words mean. As you work through each corpus, write the English word under the equivalent foreign language word, if possible. Often a word will correspond exactly with an English word, but some English words like *the* may not correspond to a word in the other language; similarly, other languages may have words which have no corresponding words in English (see p. 65).

How to use the four corpora which follow

The strategy you should use for working out the meaning and function of individual words is to compare sentences which differ minimally from each other. For example, if you were working on Madi you could take the sentences A2 and A3:

A2 otse re odi au re ra   The dog killed the chicken.

A3 otse re onya au re ra   The dog ate the chicken.

The difference in the Madi sentences is that A2 uses *odi* and A3 uses *onya*; the corresponding difference in the English translations is that A2 uses *killed* and A3 uses *ate*. So *odi* probably means 'killed' and *onya* probably means 'ate'. It would be a reasonable guess, unless you had reason to think otherwise, that *odi* and *onya* are verbs, because *killed* and *ate* are verbs too. Use this approach as a general strategy for getting to grips with the languages.

Notice that from these examples you do *not* have evidence that *otse re* means 'the dog', even though *otse re* is at the beginning of the sentence and *the dog* is at the beginning of its sentence. You can however get evidence by comparing A1 with A3:

A1 ebi re onya au re ra   The fish ate the chicken.

A3 otse re onya au re ra   The dog ate the chicken.

Since the difference here is in the word *ebi* vs. *otse* which corresponds to a difference in the translation of *fish* vs. *dog* you have good evidence that *ebi* means 'fish' and *otse* means 'dog'.

A note on the examples

Examples from languages other than English are written using the so-called 'roman' alphabet which is used for English. I have not used other standard writing systems (the Arabic examples are not written in Arabic script, for example), and I have not used anything approaching a phonetic script (tones are ignored, too). This is for convenience of sentence structure analysis, but it means that you will only get a rough sense from looking at the examples of how the words are pronounced. This is true for the examples throughout the book.

A few comments on the corpus sentences

The comments made above about transcription of words hold true also for these sentences. Only Malay has a standardized roman orthography for its words; for the other languages, the native speakers who gave me the sentences have suggested how to write the words down. Inevitably certain things are lost: Tamil for example has many spoken consonants not found in English and so is not well represented by roman letters, while Chinese and Madi are both languages in which the tone of the words is a central part of their meaning.

Because these sentences have been chosen to provide fairly simple support for the material discussed in the units (which are oriented towards English), we have avoided using complex examples, or examples which raise too many problems. The simplicity of the examples should not give the impression that the languages are in any way simple.

Adding your own language

You may know another language, in which case it would be simple to write your own list of about 30 to 50 sentences, rough equivalents to the sentences given here. You could then use these sentences in the various corpus-based exercises in this book and so adapt the end-of-unit exercises to explore this new language.

CHINESE (CANTONESE)

These examples were provided by Toh Guat Choon and Kon Yoon How. There are many different dialects within Chinese, of which the best known is probably Mandarin. The examples here are from Cantonese. As an example of differences between different dialects of Chinese, the first sentence might be:

yu sik choa kó chaet kai	A fish ate that chicken.	(Cantonese dialect)
ng sik hoi ai chaek kai	A fish ate that chicken.	(Hakka dialect)
hu chiak liau hi chiak kay	A fish ate that chicken.	(Hokkien dialect)

(The words in each dialect are in the same order; the differences here are in the word chosen for each meaning.)

Note:

    (a) Chinese has classifiers (see p. 65); *chaet* in sentence A5 is an example of one (annotated as cl.).

    (b) Chinese is a language where words are differentiated by tone (whether the voice rises, falls, etc., while saying the vowel). This is indicated for just two words below: kó and kò, to indicate that they are different words.

A Simple transitive sentence

(1) kao chui kai   A dog chases a chicken.

(2) kao sik kai   A dog eats a chicken.

(3) yu   sik   kai   A fish eats a chicken.
    fish   eat   chicken

(4) yu sik choa kai   A fish ate a chicken.

(5) yu   sik   choa kó   chaet kai   A fish ate that chicken.
    fish   eat   past that cl.   chicken

B Questions

(1) sai louchai sik choa kó teeu tai yu   Small children ate that large fish.

(2) pinko sik choa kó teeu tai yu   Who ate that large fish?

(3) sai louchai sik choa matye   What did the children eat?

(4) sai louchai yau sik choa kó teeu tai yu mo   Did the children eat that large fish?

(5) sai louchai wooi sik kó teeu tai yu mo   Will the children eat that large fish?

C Full NP compared with pronoun

(1) kó kò luiyan mai choa kó tong gau chei   That woman bought that old car.

(2) hei mai choa chei   She/he bought a car.

D Inside an NP (and attributive/predicative phrases)

(1) ngo sik choa tai teeu yu   I ate a big fish.

(2) ngo sik choa yat teeu tai yu   I ate one big fish.

(3) ngo sik choa leong teeu tai yu   I ate two big fish.

(4) ngo sik choa mui teeu yu   I ate every fish.

(5) heitei sik choa kó kò yan kei yu   They ate that man's fish.

(6) ngo taido kó kò yan   I saw that man.

(7) ngo taido li kò yan   I saw this man.

(8) kó kò yan ho seongsam   That man is very sad.

(9) yat kò ho seongsam yan sik chao mui teeu yu
     One very sad man ate every fish.

F PP

(1) ngo fong kó poon shu hai toi sheongpin
     I put that book on the desk. ('put' = present tense here.)

(2) kó poon shu hai toi sheongpin   That book is on the desk.

(3) ngo fong kó poon shu hai toi yappin   I put that book in the desk.

(4) kó poon shu hai toi yappin   That book is in the desk.

(5) hei hai okkei yappin   She is in the house.

(6) hei hai okkei chokung   She works in the house.

G Auxiliaries, tense and modals
(1) hei sik yu   He eats a fish.

(2) hei sik choa yu   He ate a fish.

(3) hei yau sik yu   He *did* eat a fish (emphasized).

(4) hei hohnang sik choa yu   He might eat a fish.

(5) hei wooi sik yu   He will eat a fish.

H *Not*
(1) kao m sik kai   A dog does not eat a chicken.

(2) hei m hohnang sik yu   He cannot eat a fish (i.e. there is no possibility of it).

J Subordinate sentence
(1) hei wa kó chaet kai ho tai   He said that chicken was very big.

(2) hei seongsam yanwai kao sei chao   He was sad because a dog died.

K Coordination
(1) kao sik choa yu tung kai   The dog ate the fish and the chicken.

L Passive

(1) kao sat choa kai   A dog killed a chicken.

(2) kai pei kao sat choa   A chicken was killed by a dog.

MADI

Madi is a language of the Central Sudanic group. It is spoken in Southern Sudan and Northern Uganda. Mairi John Blackings, the native speaker who provided these examples, speaks the Lokai dialect of Madi. The language is a tone language, which means that important information is carried in the tones on the words; however, these are not indicated in these examples. Note:

    (a) *ra* at the end of a sentence means 'definitely' (i.e. what is said is definitely true).

    (b) The pronoun subject merges with a verb, and can lead to a change in the verb; e.g. *ma* ('I') combines with *odze* ('buy') to give *madze* ('I buy').

A Simple transitive sentence

(1) ebi re onya au re ra   The fish ate the chicken.

(2) otse re odi au re ra   The dog killed the chicken.

(3) otse re onya au re ra   The dog ate the chicken.

(4) borondzi re onya ki ebi amgbugodru re ra adzini
                          The children ate the large fish yesterday.

(5) bara re onya ebi amgbugodru re ra adzini
                          The child ate the large fish yesterday.

(6) borondzi re onya ki ebi amgbugodru re ra adzini
                          The children ate the large fish yesterday.

(7) borondzi re onya ki ebi amgbugodru re adzini ra
                          The children ate the large fish yesterday.

(8) adzini borondzi re onya ki ebi amgbugodru re ra
                          The children ate the large fish yesterday.

(9) madze arabia adzini re ra   I bought the car which we spoke about yesterday.

B   Questions

(1) borondzi re onya ki ebi amgbugodru re ra adzini

                                        The children ate the large fish yesterday.

(2) adi onya ebi amgbugodru re adzini ni Who ate the large fish yesterday?

(3) adu ba onya ki ebi amgbugodru re adzini ni

                                        Which person ate the large fish yesterday?

(4) borondzi re onya ki adu adzini   What did the children eat yesterday?

(5) borondzi re onya ki ebi amgbugodru re adu nggani

                                        When did the children eat the large fish?

(6) ebi amgbugodru re, borondzi re onya adu nggani

                                        The large fish, when did the children eat it?

(7) borondzi re onya ki ebi amgbugodru re inggo

                                        Where did the children eat the large fish?

C   Full NP compared with pronoun

(1) ago re odze arabia re ra   The man bought the car.

(2) madze arabia re ra   I bought the car.

(3) mande ani adzini   I saw him/her yesterday.

(4) mande bara re adzini   I saw the child yesterday.

D   Inside an NP (and attributive/predicative phrases)

(1) ebi na amgbugodru   A fish is large.

(2) ebi re amgbugodru ambaba | The fish is very large.

(3) ebi di amgbugodru | This fish is large.

(4) manya ago re a au ra | I ate the man's chicken.

E More complex NPs
(1) madze kwe ni eno udi re ra | I bought a new picture of the tree.

(2) madze eno udi, obga laka kwe eri | I bought a new picture, drawn on it were two trees.

(3) magba kwe ni eno | I drew a picture of the tree.

F PP
(1) magba brasi si | I painted with a brush.

(2) maba buku re teremeza re ni dri | I put the book on the table.

H *Not*
(1) odi au re ku ru | The chicken was not killed.

(2) otse re odi au re ni ku | It was specifically not the *dog* which killed the chicken.

J Subordinate sentence
(1) ojo ani kemu obu | He/She said he/she comes tomorrow.

(2) ojo nyimu obu | He/She said you go tomorrow.

(3) mani ra ebi re ibwe | I know (definitely) the fish is cold.

(4) majo ebi re ibwe | I said the fish is cold.

K Coordination

(1) ama dzi arabia re pi gari re tro su ga   We took the car and bicycle to the market. (Note: *pi* means 'and', *tro* means 'with'.)

(2) ago re pi izi re tro ovu ki su ga   The man and the woman walked to the market (note the plural).

L Passive

(1) odi au re ra   The chicken was killed.

(2) au re odi ra   The chicken was killed.

(3) au re onya ra   The chicken was eaten.

(4) onya au re ra   The chicken was eaten.

M *Specifically*

(1) otse re onya au re ni   Specifically the dog ate the chicken.

N Location

(1) manya linya ra   I have eaten food.

(2) menya linya ra   I ate food (i.e. before coming).

MALAY

The examples in this section are from standard spoken Malay (Bahasa Melayu). They were provided by Wan Faiezah Megat Noordin and Yasmin Osman.

A Simple transitive sentence

(1) ikan ini telah makan ayam itu   This fish ate the chicken.

(2) anjing ini telah membunuh ayam itu   This dog killed the chicken.

(3) anjing ini telah makan ayam itu   This dog ate the chicken.

B Questions

(1) budak-budak kecil itu telah makan ikan besar itu semalam

The young children ate the large fish yesterday.

(2) semalam budak-budak kecil itu telah makan ikan besar itu

The young children ate the large fish yesterday?

(3) siapa telah makan ikan besar itu   Who ate the large fish?

(4) apa yang telah dimakan oleh budak-budak kecil itu

What was eaten by the young children?

(5) bila budak-budak itu makan ikan itu

When did the children eat the fish?

(6) adakah budak-budak kecil itu makan ikan besar itu semalam?

Did the young children eat the large fish yesterday?

C Full NP compared with pronoun

(1) lelaki itu telah beli kereta itu   The man bought the car.

(2) dia telah beli kereta itu   He bought the car.

(3) saya nampak dia   I saw him/her.

D Inside an NP (and attributive/predicative phrases)

(1) lelaki itu gembira   The man is happy.

(2) lelaki itu sedih   The man is sad.

(3) lelaki yang gembira itu makan ikan itu   The happy man ate the fish.

(4) lelaki itu makan seekor ikan yang besar   The man ate a large fish.

(5) seorang lelaki sedang makan ikan itu   A/One man is eating the fish.

(6) seorang lelaki telah makan ikan itu   A man ate the fish.

(7) dua orang lelaki telah makan seekor ayam   Two men ate a chicken.

(8) dua ekor ayam telah makan semua ikan itu   Two chickens ate all the fish.

(9) tiga ekor ayam telah makan separuh ikan itu   Three chickens ate half of the fish.

(10) kami nampak kereta lelaki ini   We saw this man's car.

F PP (and the word *ada*)

(1) saya ada buku itu   I have the book.

(2) lelaki itu ada disini   The man is here.

(3) lelaki itu ada disana   The man is over there.

(4) buku ini ada di atas meja   This book is on the desk.

(5) saya letak buku itu di atas meja   I put the book on the desk.

(6) saya letak buku itu didalam meja   I put the book inside the desk.

G Auxiliaries, tense and modals

(1) lelaki itu gembira   That/The man is happy.

(2) dulu lelaki itu gembira   That/The man used to be happy.

(3) lelaki itu dulu, gembira   That/The man used to be happy.

(4) *akan lelaki itu gembira

That/The man will be happy. (Note: an ungrammatical sentence.)

(5) lelaki itu akan gembira

That/The man will be happy.

(6) lelaki itu pasti gembira

That/The man is sure to be happy.

H *Not*
(1) anjing ini tidak makan ayam itu

This dog did not eat the chicken.

(2) anjing ini tidak akan makan ayam itu

This dog will not eat the chicken.

(3) anjing ini tidak makan ayam

This dog does not eat chicken.

J Subordinate sentence
(1) dia kata dia nampak anjing itu semalam

He said he saw the dog yesterday.

(2) dia sedih sebab dia nampak anjing itu semalam

He was sad because he saw the dog yesterday.

K Coordination
(1) saya telah makan tiga ekor ikan dan dua ekor ayam

I ate three fish and two chickens.

(2) mereka telah makan ikan atau ayam

They ate the fish or the chickens.

L Passive
(1) ayam itu telah dibunuh

The chicken was killed.

(2) ayam itu telah dibunuh oleh anjing itu

The chicken was killed by the dog.

(3) ayam itu telah dimakan

The chicken was eaten.

TAMIL

These examples are from spoken Tamil, provided by a speaker of Tamil from Malaysia (Malaysian Indian), Rajathilagam a/l Krishnan.

Note: the use of hyphens inside a word (e.g. *koli-ai*) indicates the presence of a suffix which is particularly relevant to understanding the sentence.

A Simple transitive sentence

(1) meen koli-ai saapit-ethe   *The fish* ate the chicken (i.e. emphasis on fish).

(2) koli-ai meen saapit-ethe   The fish ate *the chicken*.

(3) koli meen-ai saapit-ethe   The chicken ate the fish.

(4) nai koli-ai kondr-ethe   The dog killed the chicken.

(5) naigel koli-ai kondr-ener   The dogs killed the chicken.

(6) pillai koli-ai kondr-ethe   The child killed the chicken.

(7) pillaigel koli-ai kondr oner   The children killed the chicken.

(8) nai koli-ai saapit-ethe   The dog ate the chicken.

B Questions

(1) neetre antha pillaigel antha periya meen-ai saapit-ener
       Yesterday those children ate that big fish.

(2) yaar neetre antha periya meen-ai saapit-ethe
       Who ate that big fish yesterday? ('who' = 'which *singular* person')

(3) neetre yaar antha periya meen-ai saapit-ener
       Who ate that big fish yesterday? (here 'who' = 'which *plural* people')

(4) neetre antha periya meen-ai yaar saapit-ethe
       Who ate that big fish yesterday? ('who' = 'which *singular* person')

(5) neetre antha pillaigel yethai saapit-ener   What did the children eat yesterday?

(6) neetre yethai antha pillaigel saapit-ener   What did the children eat yesterday?

(7) yethai neetre antha pillaigel saapit-ener   What did the children eat yesterday?

(8) yeppoluthu antha pillaigel antha periya meen-ai saapit-ener

When did *the children* eat the large fish?

(9) antha pillaigel yeppoluthu antha periya meen-ai saapit-ener

When did the children eat the large fish?

(10) antha pillaigel antha periya meen-ai yeppoluthu saapit-ener

When did the children eat *the large fish*?

(11) neetre antha pillaigel antha periya meen-ai saapit-ener-aa

Did the children eat the large fish yesterday?

C Full NP compared with pronoun

(1) avaar antha gaadi-ai vaangi-naar   The man bought that car.

(2) naan antha gaadi-ai vaangi-nain   I bought that car.

(3) aval antha gaadi-ai vaangi-nal   She bought that car.

(4) neetre aval aathai vaangi-nal   She bought it (i.e. the car) yesterday.

D   Inside an NP (and attributive/predicative phrases)

(1) naan oru siriye veed-ai vaangi-nain   I bought a small house.

(2) naan oru siriye veed-ai vaangi-nain   I bought one small house.

(3) naan irandu siriye veedu-galai vaangi-nain   I bought two small houses.

(4)   naan antha miga siriye veed-ai vaangi-nain   I bought that very small house.

(5)   naan intha siriye veed-ai vaangi-nain   I bought this small house.

(6)   naan mano-vin veed-ai vaangi-nain   I bought Mano's house.

(7)   naan mano-vin siriye veed-ai vaangi-nain   I bought Mano's small house.

(8)   inthe veedu siriyethu   This house is small.

(9)   anthe veedu miga siriyethu   That house is very small.

(10)   anthe veedu konjum siriyethu   That house is quite small.

E   More complex NPs

(1) naan oru maraan-galin padathai vaangi-nain   I bought a picture of the tree.

(2) naan oru puthiya maraan-galın padathai vaangl-naln

I bought a picture of the new trees.

F   PP

(1) naan buthagathai maijain mel vaithain   I put the book on the desk.

(2) naan buthagathai maijain ullai vaithain   I put the book in the desk.

G   Auxiliaries, tense and modals

(1) meen koli-ai saapide kindrethe   The fish is eating the chicken.

(2) meen koli-ai saapide modiyum   The fish can eat chicken.

H   *Not*

(1) meen koli-ai saapide villai   The fish did not eat the chicken.

J Subordinate sentence

(1) avar sonnar naan antha koli-ye paarthathaage   He said I saw the chicken.

(2) avar naan antha koli-ye paarthathaage sonnar   He said I saw the chicken.

(3) naan antha koli-ye paartha-thaal avar-ku vartham

Because I saw the chicken he was sorry.

(4) naan antha koli-ye paarthain   I saw the chicken.

(5) nai koli-ye kondra-thaal antha pillai-ku vartham

Because the dog killed the chicken, the child was sorry.

K Coordination

(1) avar meen-ai-yum koli-ai-yum saapit-ar   He ate the fish and the chicken.

(2) meen-yum koli-yum puchigel-ai saapit-ener

The fish and the chicken ate the insects.

L Passive

(1) koli-ye nai kondr-ethe   The chicken was killed by the dog.

THE MAIN WORD CLASSES FOUND IN ENGLISH

Label	Class	Examples	Closed class?
A	adjective	rapid, blue, impossible, ultraviolet, frozen, edible, African, tiny, lovely, comical, unbelievable, snowy, former	no
Adv	adverb	well, fortunately, possibly, quickly, fast, sadly, soon, improbably, standardly, pompously, hopelessly	no
art	article	the, a, an	yes
c.c.	coordinating conjunction	and, or	yes
deg	degree modifier	very, quite, rather, somewhat, more, most, much	yes
dem	demonstrative	this, that, these, those	yes
inf	infinitive marker	to	yes
N	noun	table, action, box, unicorn, emptiness, Napoleon, postman, love, door, law, Scotland, Renaissance, cuckoo-clock	no
N	pronoun	I, me, my, you, your, he, him, his, she, her, hers, we, us, our, they, them, their, it, its, himself	yes
neg	negation	not	yes
num	numeral	one, two, fifteen, a million and two	yes
P	preposition	in, on, under, over, before, into between, to, at, beneath, for, of	yes
Q	quantifier	every, some, all, few, most, much, no, many	yes
s.c.	subordinating conjunction	that, because, whether, if	yes
V	verb	kiss, collapse, emphasize, vanish, be, deodorize, die, sit, exist, melt, build, table, vacuum-clean, window-shop	no
V_{aux}	auxiliary verb	have, be, do	yes
V_{mod}	modal verb	might, could, must, should, will, shall	yes

TESTS

The replacement test for phrase structure (p. 3)
If a sequence of words can be replaced by a single word, they may form a phrase.

The movement test for phrase structure (p. 4)
If a sequence of words can be moved as a group, they may form a phrase.

The internal structure test for phrase class (p. 20)
The class of a component of a phrase (or some other aspect of its structure) can indicate the class of the phrase.

The head rule (p. 21)
A phrase of class 'X Phrase' contains a word of class 'X' (where X stands for noun, adjective, preposition or adverb).

The position test for phrase class (p. 22)
Each class of phrase appears in certain positions, and not in others.

The replacement test for phrase class (p. 22)
A phrase can be replaced by another phrase of the same class

The affix test for word class (p. 32)
The class of a word may be shown by the possibility of attaching a particular affix to it.

INDEX